PAY

—TO—

PLAY

Sexual Harassment
American Style

TOOTIE SMITH
Treehouse Foundation

I0029779

Pay-to-Play: Sexual Harassment American Style
Published by Treehouse
Oregon City, Oregon, U.S.A.

DISCLAIMER:
The contents of this publication are intended for educational and informative use only. They are not to be considered as legal, medical or psychological advice nor as a guide to self-diagnosis or self-treatment.

WARNING:
Due to the mature nature of the contents of this book, which deals with sexual content, religious practices and political opinions, reader discretion is advised. These true stories are intended for mature audiences only.

SMITH, TOOTIE, Author
PAY-TO-PLAY
TOOTIE SMITH

Library of Congress Control Number: 2024904273

ISBN: 979-8-9901465-0-1, 979-8-9901465-2-5 (paperback)
ISBN: 979-8-9901465-3-2 (hardcover)
ISBN: 979-8-9901465-1-8 (digital)

BUSINESS & ECONOMICS / Workplace Harassment & Discrimination
POLITICAL SCIENCE / Women in Politics
SOCIAL SCIENCE / Sexual Abuse & Harassment
SELF-HELP / Post-Traumatic Stress Disorder (PTSD)

Publishing Consultant: Susie Schaefer (finishthebookpublishing.com)

QUANTITY PURCHASES: Schools, companies, professional groups, clubs, and other organizations may qualify for special terms when ordering quantities of this title. For information, email smithtootie@gmail.com.

Dedication

...for all women

My deepest gratitude to my husband, Nate,
who through his support and love,
encouraged me daily to write and gave me the freedom to do so.

Table of Contents

Acknowledgments

To my friend Laura Van Tyne, author and project manager, for her steadfast no-nonsense approach toward a sensitive subject, keeping my spirit intact, and encouragement to stay the course during the writing process.

To my fellow writer and friend, Tina Erwin, author and U.S. Navy Commander, who gave spiritual counsel and steady guidance to see the project through.

To Sam Ruckwardt, Attorney at Law, Portland, Oregon, who offered intellectual perspective and sound advice and who always takes time.

To Dr. Sarah Larson, ND, Lac, MSOM, Vancouver, Washington, for safeguarding my good health, continued friendship and a keen eye for language and medical details.

To Shelby Naylor, Mulino, Oregon, my niece, who works so hard at my other business so I don't have to.

To my dear women friends who have always stood by me through thick and thin, you know who you are. You are not afraid to tell me when you disagree with me or acknowledge my good ideas and who always love me.

Mirrors

Denise Briney Elder

The woman in the mirror looks into my eyes
Eyes that have seen sorrow and pain
Pain from broken hearts and a fractured soul
A soul that gave its last emotion.

She sees tears from her past
A past that broke her and left her empty
An emptiness she thought to never fill
A void that morphed into a black hole of despair
Her self-worth was gone as well her hope
She was looking into my eyes from my eyes.

The woman was me, the new me.

From the ashes of the pain arose a new Phoenix
A strong and confident creature
Someone who has learned from the fear
The fear that fought to control her.

I WAS abused
I WAS belittled
I WAS degraded
I WAS dead inside

It took courage and strength to get out
Out of the danger and destruction
Out of the hole I had fallen into
The hardest part is knowing
He thinks he did nothing wrong
#METOO

Quote

Courtesy of "Being a Beautiful Mess"
beingabeautifulmess.wordpress.com

"There are moments in your life
that make you and set
the course of who you're going to be.
Sometimes they're little, subtle moments.
Sometimes, they're
big moments you never saw coming.
No one asks for their life to change, but it does.
That's when you find out who you are."

Introduction

U pon reading the material within the pages of this book, you may become subject to a dazing change of thought. This altering of mind facts could propel you into making some kind of unfamiliar accomplishment that would result in improving the human condition and altering worldly events as we know them. The course of your future participation is really up to you.

The intention of this book is to amend federal law with strict punishments that can be universally applied to convicted offenders regarding , abuse and rape and to change the behavior which causes it.

Did you know at least half of all women are subjected to some type of sexual harassment in their workplaces, according to reports? But did you also know that men admit to saying or doing it to them only about a third of the time? No kidding!

You will discover these and other important truths about human interactions between the sexes within our workplace relationships sprinkled throughout the chapters of this book with never-before-heard details. The main focus of this book is sexual harassment women feel inflicted upon them by men who have power over their careers or are employed in the same workplaces. A diversion from the main point of this book -- other types of sexual harassment and the abuse that exists -- could fill volumes and would serve to dilute the essential message being conveyed on these pages. The one exception is made in Catholic Priest Sex Scandal, where during the unfolding of those particular events, I obtained a unique view from both a personal and political perspective. I included this chapter because of the life lessons we learn from it are profound.

The first step to understanding and stopping sexual harassment and abuse is to define it. The first two chapters define what we think we know and don't know about sexual harassment and pay-to-play in modern American culture and in our workplaces.

Many younger people in the workforce today are appalled at Harvey Weinstein's sexual abuse of famous actresses. But did you know the casting couch developed a worse reputation in Hollywood during your mother's and grandmother's era of growing up? In the chapter, From Hollywood to Congress: Then and Now, reveals shocking stories surrounding some of our favorite all-time actors and actresses while revealing the dirty underbelly of the people we elect to represent us.

Why do they do that? The question of why men rape and commit sexual abuse on women is explored in the fourth chapter, The Power Behind Weaponized Sex: Why Do Men Rape? with thought-provoking details.

Learn why legislating morality hasn't worked for a millennium yet our politicians keep trying to convince us by passing more and more laws in Legislating Morality.

You will learn how to stop sexual harassment in its tracks while eliciting good men to help with steps outlined in the chapter titled, The Folly of Sexual Harassment Training.

Discover ways to enhance job productivity through good practices and master essential techniques as life skills in your jobs and beyond while becoming the leader you were meant to be with examples in The Language We Use Equals the Deeds We Do.

The payouts for silence to cover up sexual harassment, abuse, and assault amounts to hundreds of millions of dollars – enough money to finance a Third World country. Just ask the Catholic Church, whose worth is billions if not trillions of dollars and who has hidden priestly sex with boys for over 2,000 years. For further historical documentation, be sure to read the Catholic Priest Sex Scandal chapter.

Why does one of America's favorite family holiday pastimes, the Macy's Thanksgiving Day Parade, find it necessary to display a massive billboard of a Victoria's Secrets ad displaying not one but two women clad only in bras during the entire 2017 two-hour show? What does that tell our youth? No wonder there is a sexual harassment problem in the American workforce today. The boundary lines have been blurred as the sex-capades seem to flourish at work while pay-to-play sets the rules for engagement. The information about this will shock your sensibilities in The Damaging Infinite Costs of Sexual Harassment and Macy's Thanksgiving Day Parade.

Finally, why is America listed as 22 out of 153 countries in world rankings for women's welfare, peace, security and inclusion while only 20 percent of us are elected to hold political positions in America? You'll see the how the failure of our time-honored societal systems has led to the frustration behind sexual harassment accusations in our workplaces in the chapter titled Why Now?

This book graphically explains the problem of sexual harassment in our workplaces. It will reveal how our brief American history has predicted the present and the reasons why so many complaints from women have arisen currently. This book will also explain how to restore our workplaces to safe havens for all while becoming prosperous and successful businesses.

Why ME to write this book? As a woman who's lived for six decades on this planet, who's enjoyed various careers as a journalist, business owner, farmer, activist and politician, I've seen and lived much. Let's face it, I fly in a man's world and I like it. In so doing, I have witnessed and felt firsthand what it means to be discriminated against or sexualized just because I am a woman. I make the case. I challenge the nay-sayers to dispute any of the well-researched studies, examinations, historical documentation and personal accounts on the pages of this book.

If anything, I am an observer and communicator. I communicate through speaking and writing and, like a journalist, I forget nothing. There are many things I'm not. I'm not a doctor, lawyer, psychologist, sociologist, accountant, famous actress, president of Fortune 100 Company or a Wall-Street tycoon. I am a daughter, wife, mother and aunt who has been elected as a State Representative and a County Commissioner. I've been owner of several corporations and a lobbyist for longer than I would like to admit tasked with influencing and changing politicians' opinions. Currently, I own a bed and breakfast in a small town in Oregon. I am a beekeeper, living on a hazelnut farm that my parents purchased as a strawberry farm in 1959 where my siblings and I grew into adults learning a strong work ethic. Thank you, Mom and Dad.

Growing up on a farm and being subjected to the unpredictability of the changing seasons instilled in me and my younger brother and sister many lessons. Opportunities present themselves only momentarily, then leave as quickly as a late spring frost can kill an entire berry crop. Preparing the crops and animals for seasonal adjustments left scant time for extracurricular activities.

Those "teachable" moments gave me strong work ethics that I carried into my jobs where I became a taskmaster. So, any engagement in on-the-job sexual endeavors was quickly thwarted as I viewed the time spent doing them as destructive, wasteful and an ultimate betrayal. For me to write about sexual harassment and the ensuing payments for silence would seem as unnatural as flying to the moon on my own wings. My marriage to my husband of over forty years should be evidence that a monogamous loving relationship is satisfying and that sexual promiscuity is a foreign concept to me.

As individuals, I believe we are each born with certain predilections anointed to us from the spirits of the Universe. We are all naturally drawn to certain vocations and professions that might seem out of the ordinary from our normal birth right and upbringing. I chose politics. I am passionate about politics. I'm a political junkie, no apologies. One day, I sincerely and humbly hope to change the world. With that in mind, the topic of this book chose me; I did not choose it.

Please embrace what you learn on the pages of this book. You will be forever changed by what and how the information is presented. Breathe it in, activate your new-found knowledge, then go forth to change your part of the world for the better.

Thank you for your conviction.

Tootie Smith

Pay-to-Play Defined

---•◦•---

Simply defined, *pay-to-play* is a phrase used for a variety of situations in which money is exchanged for services or for the privilege to engage in certain activities. The common denominator of all forms of pay-to-play is that one must pay -- giving of an item or service of value -- to "get in the game." Using the sports analogy gives the term a competitive edge, if not the appearance of an advantage that appeals to people who like to play and win at any cost, especially at politics.

It has often been said that money is the mother's milk of politics. In American politics and business, money is the driver for winning elections, obtaining power and spreading influence. Throw sex in the mix and we have fiery societal conflagration consuming media reports, as well as people's appetites for watching the mighty fall.

Fast forward to 2017, where we see an explosion of reports of sexual misconduct at epidemic proportions. It's just not the political bad boys who are getting all the attention. Business leaders, sports franchises and entertainment legends are finally being held accountable as numerous brave women come forward to tell. Pay-to-play has no longer remained a monied political game using currency but has become one of demanding sex for favors in all levels of Americana. Sex has value and therefore is established as its own form of currency. This is nothing new. What is new that it was kept quiet for so long. Pay-to-play is the new sexual harassment American style.

For this reason, sexual harassment and abuse is now being reported at all-time highs. As I write this book, on a daily basis, some form of sexual misconduct is either alleged, reported or denied at an alarming rate. The main focus of this book is sexual harassment women feel inflicted upon them by men who have power over their careers or are employed in the same workplaces. The one exception made is on the Catholic priest sex scandal, where during the unfolding of those particular events, I obtained a unique view from both a personal and political perspective. What we learn from this chapter should never ever be forgotten. One can hardly track the famous actors, business moguls or politicians who have been singled out for some sort of sexual misconduct. Continuing to keep these bad boy deeds silent is passé as women are breaking the sound barrier as they refuse to be voiceless victims.

Some men are even coming forward and voluntarily admitting to sexual missteps they may have committed decades earlier, as if by conceding to it first, they get into the queue ahead of their victims and the confession absolves them of sin.

Call me naïve, but I'm shocked if not dismayed at the volume of accounts and the famous identity of the people involved.

It remains almost unbelievable to me that here in 2018 – almost four decades after Britain's first female Prime Minister, Margaret Thatcher, was elected to run a democracy, and four and a half decades after America's women's liberation movement swept the globe – that we are fighting a battle, a women's battle over a rising tide of sexual abuse and harassment. It's as if our advanced technological and enlightened society has returned to medieval times of husbands forcing their wives to wear chastity belts while the men went off to fight wars for their kings. If reports of women are to be believed, and I do believe, *most though not all,* of the accusations made by women are true, unwanted sex claims and accusations are happening at alarming rates.

Confusion of female/male roles may lie at the root of the problem. The women's movement of the 1970's gave us permission to burn our bras and have free sex but didn't put in place new guidelines for doing so. *Just do it* was a mantra profiteered by not only Nike, but by all the willing participants. As an impressionable teen during this period of time I remember well the expectations. Title IX swept in as a new government mandate for equality for women and we were hopeful that our generation would not have to endure the same inequalities as our mothers. We were almost giddy with discovering our new-found freedom and individuality, and with it, assured success.

Advances in science and medicine produced effective birth control and allowed for free sex on demand to be enjoyed by both men and women without the fear of unwanted pregnancy. A sexual revolution swept in, but not all women participated -- after all, we had a choice. Many women chose to remain single while cohabitating with their mates. Living together outside of legal marriage became acceptable as children were born outside of wedlock. Marriage was not necessary in order to raise a family like our parents did.

Fast forward to the explosion of complaints for sexual misconduct today. One need not wonder about the confusion that exists in expectations regarding workplace behavior. Many men find no offense in their actions as women file complaints against them. After all, wasn't it a free-sex movement that gave us permission? It's as if men were given the green light to act disrespectfully toward women. Women, still not feeling the equality that was promised a generation ago, are on guard and hypersensitive as they see a failure in wage equality, a leadership void in elected office and a lack of business promotions. The result of these inequalities is men still dominate and hold most of the power in top positions of politics, business and entertainment. Women feel less empowered.

The merger of these two outlooks has erupted into daily reports of unwanted abuse as women refuse to be viewed as winged sex objects and as men are still not quite "getting" it. The perpetrators of these acts are the very men who hold real employment and economic power over the women they mistreat while failing to understand that *no* really does mean *no*.

Exploring the topic of sexual harassment is risky. It exposes us intimately to our naked mores while stripping down our moral code like never before. We talk about it happening, but can we define it? Rape, more easily defined as a violent crime, is certainly beyond what is mostly reported today as sexual harassment.

Basically, it's against the law to initiate sexual advances, or requests for sexual favors, and other verbal or physical harassment of a sexual nature. As we move forward in identifying and reporting new cases of sexual harassment, I believe this definition will be expanded upon with efforts in the U. S. Congress and other local lawmaking bodies. A more thorough discussion of lawmaking is in the chapter Legislating morality.

Margaret was kind enough to share her story with me. Her only recourse for the sexual harassment she endured at work was through her company's HR department, who chose to look the other way:

He Just Wouldn't Quit

I have worked for a large nationally chartered bank in Colorado for 19 years as a commercial banker. I have a well-established client list where I enjoy much success in bringing business and profits to this corporation. Seven years into my employment in 2005, we hired Douglas, as a lender in my department.

Within just a couple of months after his employment, Douglas started making passes at me, making constant comments about my looks and how attracted he was to me, asking me if I would go out with him. At first, I would just say no and try to ignore his behavior. He would ask to meet during work hours and ask to "rendezvous" with comments that we could go to his place for lunch. For several weeks I ignored and brushed off his comments. I would tell him I was not interested and he was making me uncomfortable, asking him to stop. His response was, "I just needed someone to teach me not to be rigid and lunch at his place would do me good."

Later on, my office sponsored a golf tournament. Douglas was assigned to the same four-person scramble team as I was. When I arrived at the golf course, he was waiting and had arranged to ride with me in my cart. Douglas insisted on driving the cart and he purposely stayed behind the other cart. As soon as we would be out of sight of others, he would put his hand on my leg telling me how nice I looked; when I would get out of the cart he would try to wrap his arms around me standing behind me and constantly whispering that I had a nice ass, saying not many women have both an ass and boobs, saying "that it was hard to find both on one woman." I continued to tell him to stop. I made it clear to him that as a co-worker I wanted our association to remain professional.

His harassment continued at the office where we both worked for months. I eventually reported Douglas's behavior to my boss. My boss was not sympathetic and told me that I must be misunderstanding something. Reluctantly, my boss talked to him.

My boss reported back to me in a couple of days and said he talked with Douglas. My boss concluded that he thought I was having a personality conflict, and it must just be a misunderstanding. Shocked, I could not believe what he was saying to me. After all of the years of employment and working together it was clear my long-time trusted boss didn't take me seriously! I felt betrayed. I began to feel my job would be in jeopardy if I were to say anything else. As a single mom with three daughters, I need this job.

Douglas became more aggressive. He would laugh when I ignored him. When I worked late, he would come into my office and try to get me to go out with him. I changed my behavior at work by altering my hours. But Douglas didn't stop. He didn't take NO for an answer. I couldn't understand why he was doing this or what his purpose in it was. The job I loved and adored so much became a stressful and difficult place.

After about six months of unsuccessful attempts in getting Douglas to quit, I told him I would report him to our human resources department, hoping that would make him stop. That turned out to be a mistake. His approach toward me changed. Douglas started to talk rudely to others about me behind my back. It escalated and I did not know how to protect myself from him. As I refused his sexual advances, he decided to go after me professionally by trying to impugn my reputation with other bank employees and even trying to steal my clients.

Douglas worked at my bank for ten years. He eventually had an affair with one of my coworkers which ended her 15-year marriage. After his employment ended, I learned of four other women at our bank that had similar experiences with him, saying they were glad he was gone. Like me, these women kept silent about his actions. My *personal assistant told me later that Douglas "had gone after me pretty hard" and that she had a difficult time getting him to stop.*

About a year ago, one of Douglas' former managers from a previous employment told me at a fundraiser that he was glad Douglas was gone. He apologized to me for having to "put up with this do nothing but chase women guy." Although I was never in this man's employment, I found it comforting that he acknowledged the happenings.

Management knew, yet did nothing. I have been in the corporate world for 19 years and I never thought I would find myself in something like this. Writing about this has brought back the terror that I thought was long ago buried. I guess it's still with me.

~Margaret

Common sense should never be lost in our attempt to define the behavior. The degree to which sexual harassment and abuse occurs can be defined as any behavior that makes one feel uncomfortable, fearful, bad or wronged and is further defined in the following chapter. Simple as that. Sexual harassment can be physical, or verbal and communicated a thousand different ways. It is always initiated. It is always unwanted. It is always felt.

While, I pretend to be no expert on the subject of sexual abuse and sexual harassment or rape, at age 61 I've lived a full life of experience in the fields of business, politics, and journalism. I've worked with men in the private sector and government and enjoyed social situations with them. My observations come through my involvement in these careers and a reflection of national events of this issue. My personal relationships with friends, with family men including my father, brother, uncles, cousins, brothers-in-law and husband, all give me a perspective that I should at least offer up a certain viewpoint for consideration.

While I don't speak for all women on this very personal and sensitive topic nor do I pretend to understand every horrid situation a woman can encounter, I can make observations and draw conclusions of where we've been historically and where we're headed for in the future of women's rights as a charter member of the majority population in this country.

Let's Get to It

I guess you could say I've been lucky: I've never been raped. Wow, that is an accomplishment! I've never felt forced to give sex in exchange for career advancement, nor would I willingly succumb to the pressure. Thank you very much. However, I have been threatened, frightened, harassed, groped, embarrassed and shunned for not participating in what I will refer to as "Sexual Pay-to-Play."

The very thought of being violently raped by a man makes me quake to the point of paralysis. It angers me to the point of wanting to commit murder against the perpetrator. And it motivates me to the point of thinking that I can actually do something to stop it. We all must fight this scourge, collectively and individually.

Have we as a human race deteriorated so far into the immoral black hole that not even our evolution from Neanderthal existence can save us? Not even society's seeming advances in behavioral leadership in both government, business, technology, medicine, social media and education has slowed this moral descent. Have our hubristic attitudes toward accomplishment and intelligence abandoned all common sense and civility to the point that the only moral imperative left is the predictable Greek tragedy sure to befall us as we struggle to keep afloat a sick society so dependent upon each other for survival, lest we sink?

At the heart of the exposure of workplace sexual harassment, are the women - the women who have been raped, harassed, and abused, who have stepped up with courageous leadership despite threats to their livelihoods, family and life itself. They risked their careers and economic existence to expose the creeps who did the dirty deeds to them. It is the heart of women who find themselves at the center of this firestorm and who will lead us out of the moral decay and hopefully to a better place. We must support them regardless of our own experiences.

As we continue with the observations, keep in mind that not all women are innocent players in this game, either. Just as not all men are rapists or abusers, not all women deserve credit for trying to clean the bathroom floor. Some women are initiators, which is not a covered topic of this book, because it is somewhat rare. Additionally, some women have inadvertently allowed sexual deviancy to continue by refusing to accept her sister's account of it or worse yet, having an attitude that just because she had to endure it, you can too. A lesson in human behavior will be revealed for sure and you may decide that our efforts so far have been pretty pathetic.

Sexual Harassment Defined

L et's be clear. Sexual harassment is wrong. Sexual harassment in the workplace is against the law. Harassment is a behavior that can be changed because it is a choice.

Identifying the term becomes important because many allegations are being made as a wide net is being cast over America's most powerful politicians, business executives, entertainers and news media moguls. The potential cost in terms of actual dollars and reputations is incalculable and will undoubtedly change the dynamic of male/female workplace relationships for years to come.

The idea of sexual harassment is a fairly modern one and the term is said to be first coined in the 1970's by women. It was used in 1973 in "Saturn's Rings," a report authored by Mary Rowe to the then-President and Chancellor of the Massachusetts Institute of Technology (MIT) about various forms of gender issues. Rowe has stated that she believes she was not the first to use the term (Rowe, Mary, 1975).

In the book, In Our Time: Memoir of a Revolution (1999), journalist Susan Brownmiller quotes Cornell University activists who in 1975 thought they had coined the term sexual harassment: "Eight of us were sitting in an office ... brainstorming about what we were going to write on posters for our speak-out. We were referring to it as 'sexual intimidation,' 'sexual coercion,' 'sexual exploitation on the job.' None of those names seemed quite right. We wanted something that embraced a whole range of subtle and un-subtle persistent behaviors. Somebody came up with 'harassment.' 'Sexual harassment!' Instantly we agreed (Brownmiller, Susan 2000).

Still, the term didn't become prominent in our language until 1991 when Clarence Thomas was nominated for the U. S. Supreme Court and Anita Hill testified against him during Senate confirmation hearings. After Hill's testimony, the number of sexual harassment cases reportedly increased by 58 percent and have been rising steadily (Bowers, Toni; Hook, Brian 2012).

Sexual harassment has become the popular term du jour used today to describe unwanted sexual advances usually toward a woman by a man as reported in thousands of news stories on television, internet and in print. However, the use of this generic term lacks punch, due to its use as a catch-all for any unwanted sexual encounters. Let's instead define sexual harassment in terms that will yield the most justice for the innocent victims involved.

The U.S Equal Employment Opportunity Commission (EEOC) says workplace sexual harassment is unwelcome sexual advances, requests for sexual favors, and other verbal or physical conduct of a sexual nature that constitute sexual harassment when the conduct affects an individual's employment, unreasonably interferes with an individual's work performance, or creates an intimidating, hostile, or offensive work environment.

Legally speaking, the accurate term is quid pro quo harassment and has a well-defined formula. Quid pro quo simply means "this for that." In the workplace, this occurs when a job benefit is directly tied to an employee submitting to unwelcome sexual advances. The action can be identified by involving some type of sexual treatment.

According to the Stop Violence Against Women website, sexual harassment occurs when: 1. job benefits, including employment, promotion, salary increases, shift or work assignments, performance expectations and other conditions of employment, are made contingent on the provision of sexual favors, usually to an employer, supervisor or agent of the employer who has the authority to make decisions about employment actions, or 2. The rejection of a sexual advance or request for sexual favors results in a tangible employment detriment, a loss of a job benefit as just described (stopvaw.org).

Many of the high profiled cases publicly reported have shown these well-established patterns of behavior. Few of these cases have not, leaving men breathing a collective sigh of relief. Once this formula is established the behavior becomes so predictable that it can be followed like leaving a trail of bread crumbs from grandmother's house. Not much originality is involved by the perpetrator. But almost all reported accounts starting with the initiation by the perpetrator, fit neatly into quid pro quo harassment. Deviations from the powerful exerting actions over the powerless are rare if one believes the news media reports – although power is not always the overwhelming defining differential, surprisingly.

The EEOC says according to their *reported* cases of workplace sexual harassment that only 51% occurred from supervisor positions. As we are discovering, most incidents go unreported. Additionally, 79% of victims are women and 21% are men, which is certainly a more predictable scenario that keeps us in line with our current belief systems.

The next logical sequence is to prove legal coercion and duress under the law. This form of harassment, coercion or duress, is often prohibited as a matter of criminal law - the crime in some cases is labeled "abuse of power" - as a form of sex discrimination or as a violation of labor or tort law (Pauldi, M. & Barickman, A .1991). Many more cases are settled out of court for money or certain other agreed to remedies in return for silence which in turn skews the quantifiable data used for reporting statistics. So therefore, to logically account for a trend in sexual harassment cases through government reports or legal court filings as always involving a power inequity, for instance, becomes problematic, as this author discovered.

Some sociologists are linking sexual harassment to workplace gender inequalities more broadly and saying it goes beyond what is generally considered as *quid pro quo* sexual harassment. A 2017 study, *Sexual Harassment, Workplace Authority, and the Paradox of Power*, defines it as:

1. unwanted touching;
2. offensive jokes, remarks, or gossip directed at the study subject;
3. offensive jokes, remarks, or gossip about others;
4. direct questioning about a subject's private life;
5. staring or invasion of a subject's personal space;
6. staring or leering at a subject in a way that made her uncomfortable; and
7. pictures, posters or other materials that the subject found offensive. (McLaughlin, Heather, 2017) If a law was adopted to include the above definition, we all could be swimming in legal hot water.

Psychologist Louise Fitzgerald and her colleagues identified behavioral dimensions of sexual harassment. Gender harassment refers to verbal and nonverbal behaviors that convey insulting, hostile, and degrading attitudes toward women such as questioning women's competence for a particular job, displaying pornography, calling women "bitches," and making obscene gestures. Unwanted sexual attention includes suggestive comments about a woman's body as well as unsolicited and unreciprocated sexual advances (Larsen, S.E. and Fitzgerald, L.F. 2010).

In a *Psychology Today* blog, Shawn M. Burn, Ph.D., writes sexual harassers may be supervisors, peers, customers, or clients. Although men sometimes experience sexual harassment (mostly young men, gay men, members of ethnic or racial minorities, and men working in female-dominated work groups), the vast majority of those who experience it are women. The EEOC estimates that between 25 and 50 percent of women have experienced sexual harassment in the workplace.

Although the focus of this book is men harassing women, both victim and the harasser can be either a woman or a man, and the victim and harasser can be the same sex. Make no mistake - sexual harassment is bullying or coercion of a sexual nature, or the unwelcome or inappropriate promise of rewards in exchange for sexual favors.

In the workplace, harassment may be considered illegal when it is so frequent or severe that it creates a hostile or offensive work environment or when it results in an adverse employment decision, such as the victim being fired or demoted, or the victim quitting the job for no discernable reason.

Sir Patrick Stewart of *Star Trek* fame strongly asserts that men bullying, harassing and even beating women is largely a *man's* problem not a woman's problem. "I know, I grew up with it." Stewart recounts that one evening when he was a child, a police officer came to their door to care for his bleeding mother.

The officer said, "Well, Mrs. Stewart, you must have provoked him - [meaning her husband]. "No, she never provoked him. He was just an unhappy, frustrated, drunken individual," Stewart reiterated (avclub.com).

Stewart, who played Captain Jean-Luc Picard in the long-running *Star Trek: The Next Generation* TV series, explained that he did not know until years later that his father came home from war in 1940 *shell shocked.* "We now know it's called PTSD, Post-Traumatic Stress Disorder, and he was never treated for it nor would he seek treatment."

Although this book limits the discussion around sexual harassment to the workplace, one can't help but wonder, how many men willingly take their domestic frustrations into their employment places. Although we must be cautious in blaming PTSD or any other mental deficiency for sexual harassment, abuse or even rape, we must be mindful that workplace sexual harassment is not isolated to just one place. Although, the workplace may be the point where we first recognize and start to treat the problem.

The following story is a prime illustration of how this abuse will follow a person throughout their lifetime. This is Mary's story:

You Know What You Have to Do

For as long as I can remember, I have had sexual advances from men. For me, it was just a fact of life growing up that you had to put up with. My earliest memories of childhood at five years old are of my father coming into my bed when my mother was called into work. This went on until I was eleven and I left his bed crying because of what he was doing to me. When he tried to get me to come back to his bed, I refused and he took my younger sister instead.

In the third grade, my bus driver would have me sit next to him and rub me between my legs. One day he took everyone home and drove to his house. I refused to get out of the bus and he finally got back in and drove me home.

My first husband had numerous affairs and gave me numerous STDs. The second time I came home and found him in my bed with another woman, I left.

When I was the assistant manager of an electronics store the district manager told me on Monday morning that he had brought a cot in over the weekend and that when it was slow we could go into the back and fool around—I told him I quit and walked out of the door.

My best friend's husband came on to me more times than I can count. One time he had taken my children and me home and when the kids went to their room, he grabbed my breasts from behind. No matter what I said he would not let me go, so I was next to the phone and called his wife and told her to tell her husband to get his hands off my boobs and to leave my house—then I put her on the phone with him.

Another time he took me to the airport so the kids could fly to their grandmother's; he waited in the car When I came back he was naked in the car. I told him when he was dressed to let me know, and I would get in.

If these stories weren't bad enough, the most career harm came to me when after years of going to college, first working on getting three masters and then my Ph.D. at Portland State University in Portland, Oregon, I had passed all the classes and exams and written my dissertation that was eventually published. All that needed to be done was to have my four advisers sign off on it. Three advisors signed off as was required, but one did not. He had me come to his office to talk with him. He had me sit in a chair; he came over to my left shoulder and rubbed himself against me. I refused to acknowledge what he was doing. Days later in class, he would look at me, in front of the entire class, and grab himself. I made sure that from that point on, I was never alone with him. While in our final meeting with my other *advisers waiting for the final sign off on my dissertation, the other advisors tried to convince him to approve my work. Still refusing, he calmly stated, "she knows what she has to do." I never gave in; I never received my Ph.D. and he was never reprimanded.*

~Mary

As more complaints about this behavior emerge, it's worth noting that the pendulum will swing wildly against any male being perceived as being more powerful over a woman who has less power. As even the slightest look or wink could be construed as harassment, it gives us all the more reason that to define it is to understand it. Gone should be the days where large institutions protect men who engage in this behavior, as evidenced by the firings of media darlings Matt Lauer and Charlie Rose to the resignations of Senator Al Franken and Rep. John Conyers, and others of the U.S. Congress. More giants will fall. Sadly enough, America's largest corporations and government entities and organizations have still failed in identifying, educating and solving workplace sexual harassment. It's hard to say why. Is it denial, lack or resources or worse yet, top management engaging in such behavior with a lack of women leadership at the top to offer a balance. Gentlemen, beware. Or better yet, help women to stop it when you hear it or see it.

From Hollywood to Congress:
Then and Now

————————◆•◆————————

I n Hollywood, California, there is an overt form of pay-to-play in
action. It's full out "give me sex, honey, or your career will never
see the light of day." The attitude in that town by some top corporate heads is, "I have the power to make you a star in my movies
and this is what I want in return." No matter that the actresses
involved have immense talent and abilities and are well paid for
their craft. As I write this, many men in the business and entertainment world are being accused of unwanted sexual advances.
Currently, the most notable is Harvey Weinstein.

Who is Harvey Weinstein and why does he matter? He matters. For the record, the very mention of Weinstein in some entertainment circles guaranteed economic and creative success in the
movie industry. Weinstein has also been accused by hundreds
of women of sexual misconduct of one form or another. He is a
prime example of bad behavior gone unchecked, ignored, and yes,
allowed to happen as his real-life sex-capades could be the source
of a fictional bad guy in any one of his own movies.

The Weinstein case is a fascinating albeit disturbing study on
sexual abuse and human behavior as some are even calling it the
Weinstein Effect. It partakes of all the essential elements to write

a textbook. The happenings at The Weinstein Company, TWC, can be duplicated at any time, place or institution in America. What has occurred at TWC has probably been duplicated elsewhere in America from the way it was covered up, the way they paid for silence and the way it made women feel.

In short, Harvey Weinstein was one of Hollywood's wealthiest and most influential career makers. As an executive producer and director of movies, he, along with his brother, Bob Weinstein, co-founded Miramax Films, which they eventually sold to Disney Films for $60 million in 1993. After that, they started The Weinstein Company, TWC, from 2005 to 2017. TWC produced hundreds of millions of dollars' worth of block buster films enjoyed by the public. In October 2017, following numerous allegations of sexual harassment, sexual assault, and rape charges against him, Weinstein was fired by his company's board of directors and expelled from the Academy of Motion Picture Arts and Sciences.

Weinstein enjoyed great success as a film maker garnering the entertainment industry's highest awards and along with them, enough money to successfully pay off all the women whom he allegedly raped, harassed and assaulted in exchange for their silence. Any actor who wanted a boost in their career would seek out Weinstein and his company for top roles.

With that much money and power, Harvey was free to do what he wanted until enough women stepped up and publicly said "Stop." There were just too many lawsuits paid by his company brought forth by women whom he abused. Even Harvey's own brother Bob, initiated the campaign to oust his own brother from the company they founded together.

Now, wait a New York minute! I just didn't fall off the hay seed truck, nor did you. We're supposed to believe that the good brother, Bob, just couldn't take his brother's immoral behavior anymore and suddenly fired him? I think not! News reports have revealed that Harvey's own employment contract with The Weinstein Company provided pay outs to women who could potentially sue him.

And we're being sold a bill of goods that his co-founder brother, Bob, the Board of Directors of TWC, company law-yers, administrators, secretaries, personal assistants and all inside staff knew nothing of his immoral behavior while it occurred and should be held harmless? The assumption is that if people closely linked to Harvey knew these atrocities were being committed then they should report them.

No doubt investigations will reveal the truth through tran-scripts of text messages, emails, and phone calls and, yes, even eye witness accounts. All these insiders are the involuntary players - who by the way made bank on the success of TWC and enjoyed economic benefits as well as fame. They allowed these sexual atrocities to occur by turning a blind eye and kept silent.

But wait, many good people indeed knew. According to reports, 16 current and former executives and assistants at Weinstein›s company said they witnessed or knew about unwanted sexual advances in the workplace or at events associated with the company›s films. Each of the 16 said his behavior was known widely throughout Miramax and the Weinstein Com-pany. Only a handful confronted him (axios.com).

Weinstein enforced a code of silence. Employees of The Weinstein Company had contracts saying "they will not criticize it or its leaders in a way that could harm its business reputation or any employee's personal reputation," a document shows. And most of the women accepting payouts agreed to confidentiality clauses prohibiting them from speaking about the deals or the events that led to them. It would appear that Weinstein, et al, methodically plotted to keep his perverted conduct a secret by paying off not only the victims, but any employee who was in a position to witness or hear about his atrocities. The tentacles of deceit and corruption were obviously widespread at TWC by using enough money, power and prestige to support most any activity that ole Harvey partook.

Were the Weinstein co-conspirators well paid to look the other way? Or were they equally coerced and intimidated into submission by Weinstein himself and the lawyers he employed to pay out hush money? This cover up affected the sexual violation of at least 80 women and counting, who have since filed complaints. Make no mistake, the silence of his troupe is a form of consent and complicity. Company culture was so strong that it enabled good people to ignore what should have been reported. The argument can be made that company culture at TWC perpetuated the role of sexual harassment.

If this type of corruption and cover-up occurred at TWC, it puts into question what other privately held companies in the entertain industry and beyond are getting away with sexual harassment, abuse and yes, even rape. Yep, pay-to-play is alive and well in the movie industry.

On a side note, Manhattan's District Attorney, Cyrus Vance, declined to prosecute Weinstein for a 2015 misdemeanor sex crime - aka rape as defined in New York statutes charge - perpetrated on Ambra Battilana Gutierrez citing prosecutorial discretion. He said that there was just not enough convincing evidence. (thenewyorker.com) In 2010, as Cyrus Vance, won the election as Manhattan's new District Attorney, he promised that "crimes committed by the affluent, the powerful, or by public officials will be investigated and prosecuted as vigorously as street crimes." Vance's critics contend that he's reluctant to prosecute a high-profile trial against a rich defendant since he tried and lost a sex case against French politician Dominique Strauss-Kahn. Vance should know, he previously received a campaign contribution from Weinstein's defense attorney, Elkan Abramowitz, also a former law partner. Will pay-to-play never end its incestuous membership into politics and law? Is it any wonder women take payouts in exchange for silence against powerful rich men? What are their options?

The fact that Weinstein got caught with his hand in the cookie jar or should we say his dick in a doorknob, is a prime example of how the powerful can fall. Certainly, other abusers engaging in the same degenerate behavior against women will be exposed as well. If the Bible is to be believed, David slew Goliath with just one well-placed stone with a handmade slingshot. Hundreds of women have taken direct aim at Weinstein. These women succeeded in bringing down this Hollywood giant to his demise as well. We are in the midst of a revolution led by women who are arming the torpedoes and ramming the gates.

Where did it start?

The casting couch: a place where professional opportunities are offered for carnal favors. As depicted in history, the well-known *casting couch* was a dominant force in the beginning of what I call today's current *sex-capades*.

The sexual abuse that occurred in the first half of 1900's Hollywood was kept secret from the public yet at the same time used to exploit women and satisfy powerful corrupt men. In a way, this historical behavior allowed for today's sexual headlines since it has never stopped.

Women were powerless back then with little economic resources at their disposal. All they had was their good looks and a budding talent. Not until the present century, have many actresses enjoyed record high salaries and gained enough economic power in their own right to leave behind the slavery of the old studio system. This new-found independence has empowered women to not only to say "no" in exchange for sex favors but to pursue criminal charges against the perpetrators unheard of in 1940, 1950 or 1960's.

Famed actor Alec Baldwin, who is known for his own missteps and verbal blunders recently said, "When women take money, [in settlement] they're silenced by money and it sets back the cause of change." Although the casting couch victims didn't regularly take money, they willingly gave sex in the hopes of landing a role in the movies. If successful, they were then paid money for acting in the movie that they gave sex for in the first place. Some desperate women succumbed to sex but were never granted the promise of the coveted movie part. Although I agree with this statement, Baldwin was severely criticized when he tried to come to the rescue. Pay-to-play was used by women to secure their own economic welfare in a highly competitive field where few were chosen and once chosen even fewer succeeded. Ruthless men used pay-to-play to feed their own sexual appetites while wielding wealth and power.

While Weinstein's revelation of decades of sexual abuses happens to be headline news, more and more women continue to come forward revealing varying acts of sexual misconduct across the spectrum of professions. The precursor to these deeds is found in our not-too-far past. If Hollywood lore is to be believed, these early days offered a road map for any powerful executive trying to satisfy his insatiable sexual appetite while offering a hungry starlet a role in his movies. Let the games of sex-capades begin while pay-to-play sets the rules.

The casting-couch tradition originated in theatrical produc-
tions on Broadway in New York well before the Hollywood film
industry became the new hub of the entertainment world. In his
book, *The Boys from Syracuse: The Shuberts' Theatrical Empire*,
Foster Hirsch details how Lee Shubert, the eldest of three brothers who helped establish Broadway's theater district in the early
1990's kept, "an elegantly furnished boudoir, reserved for leading
ladies and promising ingénues, and a shabby, spartanly furnished
room with a single couch where he met chorus girls and sou-
brettes" (Hirsch, Foster 2000). He discriminated between the
high-class women and low-class women in his sexual offerings.

Shubert may be credited with being the first to cultivate the
casting couch, but many other high-powered, wealthy men quickly
followed suit. These included but were not limited to Hollywood
legends Darryl F. Zanuck, 20th Century Pictures; Alfred Hitchcock,
Zelsnick International Pictures, Paramount; Harry Cohn, Columbia Pictures; Jack Warner, Warner Brothers; Louis B. Mayer,
Metro-Goldwyn-Meyer; and Howard Hughes, to name a few. As
famous as these creative geniuses were, so were the famous actresses
they assaulted. Marilyn Monroe, Judy Garland, Bette Davis, and
Tippi Hedren all knew too well what was expected of them in order
to advance their careers. Not all participated, however.

Louis B Mayer was said to be ruthless in his sadistic pursuit of
women. Mayer, who co-founded MGM Studios in 1924, openly
said if women failed to comply with his demands that he would
ruin their careers or they would lose their loved ones. (Variety.
com) Reportedly, Mayer assaulted Judy Garland as a teenager.
Meeting her in his office, he groped her breasts while she was
seated on his lap. (Clark, Gerald 2000).

No doubt complicity reigned during this era as Mayer used
his power and money mightily to influence, silence and buy off

would-be tattle tales. Only his secretary knew for sure what happened behind closed office doors. Publicly, he portrayed himself as a business professional with decorum and taste. Privately, he committed sexual violence on these women just before it was time to go home to his devoted wife, loving children, and a home-cooked fried chicken dinner.

As Gerald Clark points out in his book, when the studio system consolidated in the late '20s and early '30s as talkies eclipsed silent movies, the men in charge of the Big Seven notoriously abused their power. "Harry Cohn at Columbia Pictures and Jack Warner at Warner Brothers were Abusive with a capital 'A.'" Clark reveals Mayer's narcissistic attitude by stating that Mayer "believed he'd built his studio brick by brick, that it was *his* town, and *he* was king, so therefore *he* deserved all the perks of the kingdom." The perks being sex on demand with any actress who walked through the door. That was the attitude of most studio heads.

Some of these actresses, not all, participated in pay-to-play, just to get an acting role. For some, it was just a natural way of doing business. Many actresses, however, did not play and their careers suffered. Historically speaking, the proclivities of the famous *casting couch* became a way for predator men to elicit sex from actresses in exchange for the coveted Hollywood movie role.

Let's explore the bizarre behavior of producer and director Alfred Hitchcock, who reigned as a premiere movie maker of the 1940's through 1980's. His suspense movies earned him awards as he cast some of Hollywood's most famous actors from Jimmy Stewart to Janet Leigh, Cary Grant to Grace Kelly, Sean Connery to Ingrid Bergman, in his movies. Actress Tippi Hedren in her book, *Tippi: A Memoir*, details Hitchcock's sexual harassment of her while making the movies, *The Birds* and *Marnie*. Tippi Hedren is a forgotten actress who had Oscar award potential yet suffered at the hands of one of Hollywood's most successful producers.

Noted as the "Master of Suspense," Hitchcock spotted aspiring actress Tippi Hedren in 1963 in a TV commercial and promptly signed her to an exclusive long term contract, which was common for actors of that time. Tippie Hedren, mother of actress Melanie Griffith and grandmother of Dakota Johnson, also tells about the abuse in the autobiographical 2012 HBO movie, *The Girl*, starring Sienna Miller.

Hitchcock's abusive behavior began when he cast Hedren in *The Birds*, her first film and Hitchcock's follow-up to famous movie, *Psycho*, starring Janet Leigh. While starring in *The Birds*, Hedren says Hitchcock grabbed her, attempted to kiss her and had a secret door installed between his office and her dressing room, which he entered at will while she occupied it (Hedren, Tippi 2016).

Throughout their four-year working career together Hedren describes his method of operation to ensure her compliance while viewing her as a sexual conquest. She repeatedly refused his advances but paid the price as he controlled her career by refusing contract concessions to work in other movies at other studios. In essence, Hitchcock owned Hedren's career through the exclusive contract she signed which was not voidable at the time.

She claims he once threw himself on top of her and tried to kiss her while they were travelling in his limousine. The next day on set, while filming the famous phone booth scene in the movie, *The Birds*, in which Hedren's character is attacked by birds, she says one of the mechanical crows broke the supposedly shatter-proof glass, shards of which hit her in the face. She also says that in a scene where her character was attacked by birds in a bedroom, she was told the mechanical birds would not work, and that they would have to use live ones (thedailymail.co.uk).

She purportedly spent five days filming the scene with the live birds being thrown at her and attached to her body with elastic bands. Hedren says she broke down when a bird that had been attached to her shoulder almost pecked her in the eye, and she spent the following week in bed, exhausted. Hedren suspects that Hitchcock was attempting to punish her for rebuffing his sexual advances.

Hedren writes in her autobiography, that he expressed his love for her directly, although they were both married at the time. Hitchcock would "find some way to express his obsession with me, as if I owed it to him to reciprocate somehow." One day, Hedren says, he summoned her to his office. "He suddenly grabbed me and put his hands on me. It was sexual, it was perverse, and it was ugly," she writes.

Hitchcock reportedly grew frustrated at her resistance and threatened to ruin her career. Hedren says he blocked Universal Studio when it wanted to submit her performance for an Oscar and talked disparagingly of her to others. Hedren alleges that the director ordered other cast members not to socialize with her or touch her and grew petulant if he saw her talking to other men.

She was still under contract to him for two more years, and Hitchcock refused to allow her to take work with other directors. This, combined with other studios' reluctance to antagonize Hitchcock - a very rich and powerful movie executive - meant her career suffered and never recovered.

"Studios were the power," Hedren said in 2012. "And I was at the end of that, and there was absolutely nothing I could do legally whatsoever. There were no laws about this kind of a situation. If this had happened today, I would be a very rich woman."

Hedren, now in her late eighties' says she is compelled to tell her story. She concludes, "Of course, sexual harassment still occurs, but there are far more safeguards in place to prevent it, far more awareness and knowledge of the dangers. In my day, the casting couch was in regular use. It was accepted, as a matter of course, that actresses would have to do certain things to get certain parts and nobody found it that surprising."

Hedren's abuse was not an isolated incident. According to Tim Oglethorpe, for DailyMail.com, director Sir Alfred Hitchcock was a sadistic sexual predator who devoted his 40-year career to making stars of ice-cool blondes. "He would become fixated, fall hopelessly in love and, using his powerful position in Hollywood, try to woo them into bed via the casting couch." And whether he succeeded or failed, Hitchcock would bully them ruthlessly. Among them were favorites Joan Fontaine, Kim Novak, Janet Leigh and — his greatest infatuation of all — Grace Kelly, who later became Princess Grace of Monaco (thedailymail.co.uk).

This wrong behavior knows no boundaries as we explore the numerous and wide-spread sexual harassment claims at hand. Substitute sex for money as a currency - something of value to some people - for some tangible item of value in return and you create your own brand of pay-to-play. Pay-to-play is alive and well for those who demand sex in return for granting an acting role, a job promotion, political favors and political contributions. I believe there's not a sector in American society today that hasn't been stained by pay-to-play sexual harassment.

As I write this, in just one hour on my local morning news cast, there are five more potential cases of sexual abuse reported as if these occurrences were as common as another car wreck during morning rush-hour traffic.

The first was an update on dirty politician, former Congressman Anthony Weiner who after a decade of sending naked pictures of his genitals to underage innocent women was finally convicted for exposing himself to a 15-year-old girl via a text. Finally, officials were convinced a crime had been committed. Just how many times did this perp send photos of his penis to girls before authorities were convinced to charge him with a crime? Was it because they didn't know what to do or was it that there was no law on the books under which to prosecute this behavior as a crime? Ultimately, Weiner will serve 21 months in jail, "get counseling" and be put on parole for three years. Weiner's sick behavior is just the first of many high-powered politicians that will be revealed as more women come forward.

Second, famed Oscar winner, writer, actor and director Ben Affleck who issued an apology for groping actress Hillary Barton in 2003 on camera in an interview with the Associated Press. This apology came after many rumors of Affleck's unseemly behavior with other women. Obviously, he's trying to get out in front of what undoubtedly could become multiple claims against him as well.

Third, Kevin Spacey, famed actor and producer of the popular Netflix series *House of Cards*, has been ousted from starring in his own series and fired from future Netflix movies for attempting to molest a 14-year-old boy. Netflix couldn't cut its ties to Spacey fast enough.

Charlie Rose of CBS and OPB fame has been fired after a *Washington Post* exposé outlining decades of his lewd sexual mistreatment of women. (WashingtonPost.com) Matt Lauer, *Today Show* co-host for decades, was fired after a woman brought forth evidence of his vile sexual harassment. Famed actor Dustin Hoffman as well is said to have sexually harassed very young girls over the course of his career.

Who is Jeffery Lane? The local Portland ABC affiliate on November 10, 2017 morning's news broadcast reported this villain was finally arrested by Multnomah County, Oregon, sheriff's deputies after the local district attorney's office gathered enough evidence of sexual abuse when he followed women into an elevator at a local shopping mall. He was charged with sexual assault and kidnapping. Fortunately, the women escaped and were able to help authorities capture the pervert (ABC News Affiliate, KATU 2).

Stories like these have existed for years and have been ignored by all media outlets for decades, as well. Finally, not even the news media can turn a blind eye to the overwhelming volume of sexual harassment accusations. They are at last reporting on what women have been saying for years, if not decades. Where this industry has refused to report sexual harassment deeming it too distasteful, or chose not to believe the women, or whether it was too afraid of losing its advertising revenues by reporting, one can't be sure. But at least there is now enough communal awareness, that these stories are being told. Law enforcement officials must find ways to prosecute without impunity. Settling unnamed lawsuits that promise huge sums of money in exchange for silence should be viewed as adding to a corrupt system of pay-to-play yet redefined. Men pay so they can go play some more, undetected.

While women of Hollywood and the entertainment industry were the first to bravely come forward, our sisters in the political world are also joining the chorus, and rightfully so. However, the political profession is very different, - not any better, just different - and people need to understand that the rules hold female politicians to a double standard. And, if you are a woman of color, a triple standard exists. Women who are elected to public office in these leadership positions risk being fired by their constituents just for talking publicly about the taboo subject of sexual abuse.

Can you imagine your favorite woman politician, the one whom you admired and trusted to vote for *your* value system and keeper of your pocket book as well, interviewed on the nightly TV news, describing the graphic details of a sexual invasion on her body? Pervasive thinking by the public coupled with the conventional wisdom of the day says that she must have done something wrong to bring on this behavior. Women are especially notorious in this belief as I have had some women say to me privately: "So, Tootie, what did you say to bring this on?" This is a familiar retort I received when privately confiding to my political "friends." It's especially true if you are, like me, a strong, vociferous person known to speak up for the disenfranchised. This underlying attitude in the public keeps good women from wanting to run for office. Because historically, in the end, the perpetrator will deny the accusation, the authorities will make you prove it before they investigate, and the voting public brands you a hussy. Thank God that is all changing, but not fast enough. Fighting back is not attractive for women, but we must do it.

In Hollywood, TV shows and movies glamorize such behavior and actresses can win an Oscar for her betrayal as a rape victim. So logically speaking, actresses risk less with movie goers who pay ticket fees than do elected politicians whose voters weigh every conceivable reason to throw the incumbent out of office. Just listen to their opponents' accusations during election season, whether true or not. In America, we still place women politicians on a higher moral pedestal while at the same time waiting for them to fall. Besides who would elect a woman who admitted to being hurt by a rapist or sexual harassment as president? It would be viewed that if she wasn't strong enough to stand up to her assaulter, then she isn't strong enough defend America against its world enemies. Talk about a double standard!

Unlike Hollywood, politics is a profession that still prides itself on at least the resemblance of decorum and proper behavior. Regardless if you are a Republican or Democrat, liberal, moderate or conservative, there still exists a cloak of conservatism that is a standard for comportment for women politicians. For women to openly admit that as victims they were somehow willing or unwilling participants in deviant behavior, well, it sends a fickle voting constituency to potentially think "let's elect us a "clean" representative who hasn't admitted to being involved in a sexual scandal." Good luck in finding one.

Currently, I know or have heard of many women in the political arena here in Oregon - whether it be elected politician or lobbyist or other public service - who haven't been on the receiving end of an unwanted sexual aggression at one time or another. There is still a bit of accusatory blame attached by women to a woman who admits to being on the receiving end of sexual harassment. People's perception is everything in politics, no matter how misguided, because the public makes decisions and ultimately votes upon what they *perceive* to be true, not what is actually true.

In America, political figures are the closest to royalty as we get. And as we know from England's royal family, scandal is taboo, shunned and forbidden. Scandals are as distasteful to royal followers as a politician's local voting bloc in America.

National male politicians, right and left, Republican and Democrat, are seeing more claims of sexual misconduct of one form or another brought against them. A few are refuting the charges and some are resigning from office, and some are apologizing claiming ignorance. Did they not get the memo? These are the very people elected who passed antidiscrimination laws. Most of the current congressional members of 2017 U.S. Congress who have been accused, were present in the Congressional body when

Title IX was upgraded in 2011 to include sexual harassment as an illegal act. They all knew the implications of the potential criminal action. The sexual abuse of their disempowered employees and elected women officials occurs in both chambers of the U.S. Congress without discernment.

With that in mind, currently many women members of Congress have come forward admitting for the first time that sexual harassment exists for themselves or staffers. I applaud their efforts as one who knows the inherent risk of admitting to being subject to unwanted invasions of their person and the accompanying guilt and shame that goes with it. The potential for public ridicule is great. The fallout of such revelations has yet to be measured. It's hard, embarrassing and infuriating, yet cleansing all at the same time. No woman wants to relive the humiliation and shame while being exposed to once again a potential disapproving public.

The Power Behind Weaponized Sex: Why Do Men Rape?

Why *do men rape women?* Let's ask that question in a more qualifying light. *Why do some men — a very small segment of the male population — inflict the cruelty of rape on women?* But greater in numbers, why do some men think sexual mistreatment, harassment or abuse of women is acceptable?

For the record, sex used as a weapon is as old as civilization. Ancient armies using rape to conquer and impregnate women during battles is well-documented throughout time. What makes it seem to shock now is that we assumed that we have evolved past this barbaric time in human evolution. But have we?

Psychologists, psychiatrists and mental health sex experts have written volumes on the subject. As a lay person asking the question, I chose to center the discussion of this book to American society, and specifically the fields of politics, business and entertainment. These three arenas are areas where a huge power differential exists between men who have always controlled the oxygen in the atmosphere and where women seek to break the glass ceiling allowing more of us to breath.

Again, let me be clear: I'm no expert nor am I a trained professional psychiatrist, but one does not need to have access to a library full of psychology books filled with detailed writings from doctors and PhD's to dissect the complicated mind in relation to the physiological responses necessary to perform these hideous acts.

My observation, like most women, comes from living on this planet for more than 60 years. As an elected policy-maker, I had a front row seat into human behavior and was charged with decision making when people's actions went bad. As a writer, I have read, interviewed and observed behaviors and naturally drawn conclusions. As business owner, I was acutely aware of the cost sexual misconduct yields.

At the risk of being criticized for oversimplifying, I offer the following, not as a final conclusion on human behavior in a complex society, but simply as a submission of ideas for discussion so that we all can begin to find answers.

Inherent at the core of this revolution of awareness of sexual mistreatment is the difference between men and women's anatomy, which is often misunderstood. Men see their penises as an active means to an end. Women see their vaginas as an untouchable holy shrine. Since birth, boys have viewed their penis with pride and joy always visible always omnipresent. On the other hand, girls slowly came to realize their vaginas even existed while buried internally with how many other organs of pleasure and function. We can't see it but we know it's there. Men willingly abdicated their power with the betrayal of the very muscle that makes them unique, their penis. Women felt their center was destroyed as the shrine sanctity of a woman's unique sexuality was not respected, their vagina.

Plainly put, men do it – rape - because they can. Men do it because they can. If you didn't understand it the first two times, men rape,

use sex as a weapon because they can. They are uniquely equipped both physically and socially.
They have the anatomy.
They have the immorality.
They have power.

In other words, they do it because they can in the absence of an effort to stop them. Let's explore further. In the legal profession of prosecuting crimes there are three essential elements needed to successfully prove someone's guilt of a crime: *means, motive* and *opportunity* (Psychology Today).
First, *means* is defined as having the tools necessary to commit the crime. In a man's case, his *means* is his unique anatomy which women do not possess. Second, *motive* is defined as the reason or actual idea or possession of immorality where no morals exist. And lastly, *opportunity* is the absolute power these men execute over women. It can be physical power of strength or surprise or the power of wealth and influence. All this will be discussed later in this book.

Simply put:
They have the anatomy which is *means.*
They have the immorality which is *motive.*
They have power which is *opportunity.*

Ironically, for most men and women alike, strict taboos against rape still exist except for the person who performs the act. The thought repels us. Until recently, the act remains buried and ignored despite efforts of its few victims to give it attention by reporting it to authorities. This epiphany of bad behavior comes at a time when governments and businesses alike have increased the mandatory training courses in their workplaces on diversity, respect of others, and appropriateness of all things human.

However, in places like Hollywood where no HR department exists, it's a Wild West show of immorality, too much money and centralized power. The United States Congress has no excuse. Their only defense is not enough women were elected to keep them clean and honorable. Whose fault is that? This old boys' club privately jokes about "doing it" like locker room chatter of high schoolers while at the same time holding the keys that make the very laws that would start to cure the problem.

For the purist who seek academic affirmation, I can cite several authorities where my theory of *anatomy, power and immorality* trifecta is given credence.

According to psychologist Melissa Burkley, Ph.D., men rape and harass because it's in their brains (and I would argue that in the absence of their unique anatomy they would lose their ability to rape. After all, women do not have the ability to poke or fling their genitals in places where they are uninvited and recorded cases of women instigated rape, though they exist, are very rare.) She quotes her own research that shows where men are encouraged to see themselves as predators, they will then see their mate as prey (psychologytoday.com). Although to be fair to the sexes, women are capable of rape just as easily as men – absent a penis – by causing arousal in younger males or boys. The topic of this book however, is the rape, sexual assault and harassment perpetrated by men upon women. The former objectionable behavior could be the subject of volumes as a distinctly rarer topic.

Burkley and her colleagues decided to test whether this men-as-predator and women-as-prey metaphor of dating is harmless or not. In their study, men and women of varying ages read a passage that described a man on a first date with a woman. Half of the participants were randomly assigned to read a neutral version of this story. The other half read a version that included several references to the men-as-predator and women-as-prey metaphor. For example, instead of referring to a "night on the town," the metaphor version stated, "a night on the prowl." And rather than saying he "enjoyed the get-to-know-you phase" of dating, the metaphor version stated he "enjoyed the chase."

After the reading, all participants completed questionnaires designed to measure their attitudes about rape. The results indicated that there was no significant difference for women who read the neutral and metaphor versions of the reading. But the results for the men in their study was quite different. Men who read the metaphor-laced reading were significantly higher in their beliefs that perpetuate rape (e.g., women who are raped while drunk or sexily dressed asked for it; if a girl doesn't fight back it's not rape; women often lie about being raped) than men who read the neutral reading. Similarly, men who read the metaphor version were also more likely to indicate they would engage in rape if given the chance.

Although more work needs to be done on this theory, there is enough evidence to suggest that not much human evolution has taken place despite the assumption that we are now living in a much more sophisticated and moral society.

Ronald E Riggio Ph.D., talks about how power plays a role in sexual harassment in his article, "The Minds of Powerful Sexual Predators: How Power Corrupts." Simply, Riggio explains the three factors he believes propel powerful men to perform outrageous behavior. They are *Social Dominance, Exception-Making and Just Being Male* (psychologytoday.com).

He says *Social Dominance* is the notion that powerful, or more dominant, hierarchies develop in societies, such as men over women, whites over people of color, rich over poor, and the belief that they are superior and their victims are lesser in stature. The identity of such is real and as old as the ages.

His second theory, *Exception Making* is the most dangerous for those of us seeking a change in behavior. Riggio says, "*Exception Making* is a common reason why power corrupts." Powerful individuals begin to believe that the social rules and laws that govern other people (those "lower" classes) don't apply to them because of their [lack of] status and power. This is reinforced when the powerful individual can use money or influence to keep from being discovered, or to "settle" with victims. This also may be the main reason that harassment training has proven ineffective. A more thorough review of sexual harassment training is discussed in the chapter, The Folly of Sexual Harassment Trainings.

In his book, *Just Being Male*, Riggio validates the penis anatomy theory. Riggio gives credit to researcher John Antonakis and his colleagues in recent series of studies published in *The Leadership Quarterly*. This study measured degrees of honesty, personality and testosterone in male leaders. The only significant predictor of corruption was the level of testosterone in the leaders, and, as you might suspect, women, who have lower levels of testosterone, were more resistant to corruption than were the male leaders (Bendahan, S., Zehnder, C., Pralong, F.P., & Antonakis, J. 2014).

Riggio concludes that over time leaders may begin to believe that they are "above the law," and that they are entitled to receive more and more (and that low power people deserve less). There is substantial evidence of the corrupting effect of power. As a lay person running in the fields of politics and business, I couldn't have said it better myself!

The final authority I will cite is Shawn M. Burn, Ph.D., who in her article "What Do Psychologists Say About Sexual Harassment?" details the causes and effects of sexual harassment.

From a feminist psychological perspective, Burn says sexual harassment arises from traditional expectations and relationships between the genders that overflow into the workplace although they are irrelevant or inappropriate. It's conceptualized as being about power, who has it and who doesn't have it.

"Because it [sexual harassment] intimidates and discourages women in the workplace, it reinforces workplace gender hierarchies of privileged men. Some men abuse their organizational power to sexually coerce or intimidate women and to allow sexual harassment to occur unabated" (psychologytoday.com).

Burns also makes the argument that organizational reform must happen for society to get past this abuse. Although not wholly positive this will happen soon it may take generations to accomplish. This gives credit to my argument that men must control themselves and their anatomy and that behavior is a choice.

Further statistical analysis reveals some troubling thinking by our male work-place colleagues. A study done by Morning Consult for the New York Times in November 2017 asked 615 men about how they conduct themselves at work reveals insights. Nearly one third of men who self-reported said, "they had done something at work within the past year that would qualify as objectionable behavior or sexual harassment." (nytimes.com) The survey also concluded that many of the men lied when failing to admit if they engaged in such activities. The most common type of action is what researchers call gender harassment. This includes telling crude jokes or stories and sharing inappropriate videos. About 25 percent of men in the survey said they had done at least one of these things. Concurrently, women said they felt sexually harassed 50 percent of the time.

An additional study from the non-profit CARE, an organization founded in 1945 that fights global poverty, supports similar conclusions. CARE surveyed 9,408 men in 8 countries and found that nearly a quarter of men (23%) think it's sometimes or always acceptable for an employer to ask or expect an employee to have intimate interactions such as sex with them. Countries surveyed by the Harris poll are Australia, Ecuador, Egypt, India, South Africa, the United States, the United Kingdom and Vietnam. The figure was highest in Egypt, where 62 percent of men said it's sometimes or always okay for employers to ask or expect intimate relations from employees.

"Being expected to have sex with your employer – that's not a job description, it's sexual abuse," said Michelle Nunn, CARE's president and CEO. "And it speaks to the global epidemic of harassment and abuse in our workplaces."

CARE commissioned the survey to better understand the often-unspoken rules and perceptions that underlie sexual harassment worldwide. It found wide gaps between what men and women find acceptable at work in most countries surveyed. In the U.S., for example, 44 percent of men age 18-34 say it's sometimes or always acceptable to tell a sexual joke to a colleague at work while only 22 percent of women in that age group do. In India, 52 percent of men say it's acceptable to rank colleagues based on their appearance.

"We need more organizations to proactively create anti-harassment cultures accompanied by strong managerial support," said Burns. "Right now, it is downright sad that many affected women feel they have to put up with sexual harassment in the workplace. We don't want to hurt our careers or harm relationships. We anticipate retaliation and need our jobs. We know colleagues, supervisors, or CEOs won't support us and that we will become pariahs in our workplace. Pursuing legal avenues of redress is untenable given the high personal and financial costs."

Legislating Morality

As I write this, currently many successfully elected women in our U.S. Congress are coming forward with sexual harassment stories during their careers. In the field of politics where money and power reign supreme from men at the top, the more appropriate question to ask is – What woman in politics *hasn't* been sexually harassed while on the path to successful election? Or even after their election, during their term of service? The question is as important as the air we breathe. My personal experience offers tribute to their sentiment. But I'm not writing this book to talk about me.

In so telling their stories they are trying to strengthen laws against the sexual misconduct done to women. My hat's off in their courageous efforts. We must succeed. The big reveal in all this is the deep-set attitudes regarding sexual harassment toward women in general that has become obvious as more scandals are revealed. The younger generations of women in the workplace are shocked that it even exits while the older generations of women in the workforce are aware but hoped an evolution took place. The evolution has not happened. It's as if we exist in two alternate universes: The first is the expectation of a sex-harassment-free workplace; the second is realization there are workplaces where it flourishes.

Certainly, new legislation will be written with all good intentions to fix this sexual morality crisis America finds herself in and rightfully so. The issue must be addressed in our courts and at the highest levels of law-making possible. However, I fear all these good intentions could fall by the wayside. Why? Because we already have rape laws on the books, but do we really?

For most of our modern history, rape was defined as a property crime, not an offense against women. Rich, male plantation owners used slaves for labor and sex on demand since they held the ultimate power that went unchallenged.

Rape charges by a black slave woman, for instance, never were brought to the light of day since the assault occurred by their powerful, white, rich owners. After all, black women were their "property."

In some cultures, rape was seen less as a crime against a particular girl or woman than as a crime against the head of the household or against chastity. The penalty for rape was often a fine, payable to the father or the husband, as they were in charge of household economy. That assumption begs the question: does that make the rape acceptable since you paid for it? Or should we call it what it really is - legalized prostitution?

This brief history lesson brings up a formidable point - rape wasn't even characterized as a crime until the 1970s. The women's liberation movement brought forth changes in the perception of sexual assault. Rape was finally viewed as a crime of power and control rather than purely of sex, due in large part to the female outrage at the time.

Since few women were elected in the male-dominated Congress of the 1970's, actual reform was left to state legislatures. Federally rape and assault laws lack the punch necessary for prosecutors to convict. Instead, each state has their own laws. These definitions can vary considerably, but many of them do not use the term *rape* anymore. Instead, they use words to intentionally dilute the violence of rape such as sexual assault, criminal sexual conduct, sexual abuse, and sexual battery. Many states have also ignored force, violence and consent as a factor in rape instead choosing to focus on the sex act and age as a component. (cga. ct.gov) Fast forward to 2017 when so many accusations are forthcoming. It gives us little hope that sexual abuse, assault, or misconduct has a chance of prosecution in our courts, let alone trying to define the term, *sexual harassment*. So is it any wonder that the same overseers - the people who write our laws - have failed in their attempts to define the term rape.

It is still shocking to me personally that, according to RAINN, Rape and Sexual Assault Crime Definitions, in 2016 half of the states in America failed to legally define rape as a crime. This presents another huge hurdle to women in Congress who want to strengthen laws around rape, sexual assault, abuse and misconduct (apps.rainn.org).

Let's look at Roy Moore, the Republican nominee for U.S. Senate in Alabama's special election to replace Jeff Sessions, who was appointed to Attorney General in the Trump administration. Moore has been accused of having sex with 13- and 14-year-old girls when he was in his thirties. He denies the claims and says he passed a lie detector test. He's 70 now. Do the math. Moore would have allegedly committed sexual assault back when Alabama's rape laws did not speak to the illegality of having sex with underage girls. Yes, of course if true it's disgusting and perverted, but I bet it was a more common practice in some states than the folks would ever want to admit today. Many of the attitudes of men today are the same as back then, yet women have expected men to evolve their thinking alongside their own views of sexual harassment. Evolution is not on a fast track regarding male sexual thinking. Moore lost his bid to win a seat in Alabama amid objections of over 20 sitting Republican U.S. Senators who demanded he quit the race.

Incumbent Democrat Senator Al Franken of Minnesota was accused of groping women while in his previous life as a comedian and as an elected U.S. Senator. His awe shucks, forgive me Mom, little boy apology temporarily endeared himself to his true believers as he claims he just didn't remember if his hands were full of some woman's ass. Franken was smart enough to know that being rebellious just doesn't work and has fully employed the art of repentance in the tone of his apologies.

"I can't say that it hasn't happened," said Franken in a CBS *Today Show* interview with Esme Murphy on November 27, 2017. "I take thousands of pictures and its always chaotic. I'm very sorry *if* these women experienced that." Really? He basically called these women liars. And by the way, Franken is also known for his keen mind and memory of details when crafting legislation. This is such BS! For the record, I have had hundreds of photo ops in my political career – granted nothing in volume compared to Franken – but I would definitely remember if I took a handful of testicles, even just once. Just saying. For the record, I have never groped men. In the end, Franken couldn't battle most of his democrat colleagues in the Senate who demanded his resignation. He resigned from U.S. Senate on December 7, 2017, speaking to an empty Senate chamber.

It would seem that U.S. Congress has its work cut out for itself. While some lawmakers will rush in with solutions to be codified in law, others will turn to behavior modification through sexual harassment training for all members of Congress and their staff. Sexual harassment trainings are discussed in the chapter, The Folly of Sexual Harassment Trainings.

"The first hurdle is trying to legally DEFINE rape. Our greatest institutions have tried: FBI's Uniform Crime Report, the United States Armed Forces Uniform Code of Military Justice, and the U.S. Supreme Court have all weighed in to add to the definition. Yet we still lack a universal definition codified in federal statute such as murder and kidnapping, which both carry well-defined federal punishments. Despite the failures of the past Congresses to codify rape, they must now move forward to give not only rape but all sexual crimes equal status. Failing to define the heinous crime of rape holds America hostage to its own form of immorality.

As long as rape is currently viewed as acts against women, the criminal act will not rise to the status or importance given to other national issues of concern such as healthcare, immigration or budgeting. Instead, rape and sexual abuse should be viewed as an assault against all humanity and as a threat to national security since it potentially affects over half of the U.S population - women -- and untold children. In failing to DEFINE rape, then what possible hope can we place upon our lawmaking body to assure that sexual harassment in the workplace can be cured? Let's not be blinded by the fact that the historically male-dominated U.S. Congress has refused to take such actions despite the fact that the U. S. armed forces are fighting this very battle internally which in turn threatens to weaken our protective forces. Sex crimes eat away at the very fabric of human dignity and weakens a person's reserve, thereby weakening our society, thereby weakening America's resolve to maintain its status as the humanitarian leader of the free world.

The difficulty in passing such legislation is not lost on the complexities involved. My experience as law maker would be to take each component part of rape such as --consent, age, violence, the act as in penetration, punishment, law enforcement, jurisdictions, and penalties, and any other evolving factors -- in parcels until a complete body of work is defined. Taking on this ground-breaking legislation through thoughtful piecemeal assembly will set the tone for a healthier and more prosperous humanity whereas laws like health care, tax and immigration reform and building a wall will fail because those efforts, while noble, are just mere adjustments at nibbling around the edges of what really ales the human soul.

Additionally, addressing the element of "consent" is critical in determining whether conduct of rape and sexual assault statutes is criminal. Many of the accused men use the defense that the sex they are accused of was consensual. The women involved argue the opposite. Conventional wisdom now tells us that just because consent was given once, that does not mean permission is extended to subsequent encounters. Non-consensual sex is further divided into factors related to the circumstances of the assault, that is, did the victim communicate her unwillingness to participate in sexual activity, and other factors related to the victim, such as age and relationship (Anderson, Michelle 2003).

In their paper on "Rape and Sexual Assault in the Legal System," presented to the National Research Council of the National Academies on Sex, Carol E. Tracy, Terry L. Fromson, Women's Law Project Jennifer Gentile Long, and Charlene Whitman, conclude that crimes of sex are a set of complex dynamics that call for detail-oriented investigations and statutory analyses. Sex offenders often employ unique, manipulative, and murky methods in order to victimize.

Some local jurisdictions have updated their laws to include our ever-expanding knowledge of rape, sexual assault and offender behaviors. In other jurisdictions, the laws remain sadly outdated in either language or content. It appears that a huge disconnect exists between the law and reality. Who will lawmakers listen to when making new laws? A rare effort of collaboration between victims, experts in sex crimes, offender and victim behaviorists, legal professors, justice and law officials, medical and psychological counselors and government bureaucrats need to diligently help pen effective legislation that will work.

We have laws against murder, yet murder happens. It's the same with driving while under the influence. People still insist on driving while drunk. How do we persuade people to change their behavior? In particular, what kind of societal attitudinal change needs to happen to keep men from abusing and harassing women in the workplace?

These future efforts by Congress and state legislatures to strengthen laws reminds me of an experience I had along my way through my metamorphosis of political growth as an elected legislator.

A very valuable lesson came my way when I as 43-year old naive state legislator first elected to the Oregon House of Representatives in 2001. One of the positives about running a campaign is the chance to make friends with people whom you normally wouldn't have the opportunity to meet. The wealth of information and the breadth of opinion available to me was wide. For the most part, my associations with lobbyists, campaign workers, consultants, staffers and state employees were positive. There were many people whom I can refer to as credit for my knowledge base and growth, but for the purposes of discussion on this topic, I'll refer to my friend, Ted.

Now, Ted would not have been a stand-out in my mind except for the fact that he was so kind to me, genuinely so, when I first decided to run for office. I first met him through the usual list of people who were willing to support my campaign because we shared the same belief system. In other words, my Republican caucus told me he was a good guy.

Ted was older and a true gentleman and one of the most experienced influencers around. Yes, he was a lobbyist. He was patient and took the time to school me on the history of Oregon State Legislature, which I later used to my advantage in passing laws.

This wise, self-educated man, despite the fact he was a lobbyist, became one of my de facto mentors. For the record, not all lobbyists are wicked money grubbing bottom feeders. He warned me whom to watch out for and whom to befriend. As I learned, his information was usually right.

He once advised me during a heated emotional discussion about a bill I was going to write that directly dealt with changing a human behavior. I was passionate about my issue and I knew I was right and would win not only the support of my colleagues who would vote for it but that of my constituents as well. He came to me one day and started a casual conversation, asked me why I was doing it.

Dumbfounded, I indignantly responded, "There are so many wrongs being committed in the world. This needs to be fixed and now." My thinking was to hurry up and change the world immediately by passing a law that would no doubt improve life in general for anybody affected.

The longer we talked the more I realized Ted was becoming a little frustrated with me. He finally said, "You can't legislate morality, Tootie!" It took a while for that statement to sink into my ambitious, fertile mind. "Think about it," said Ted. "Since the Romans organized the first world government, mankind has been trying to pass laws to stop this or do that. It just doesn't work. Some people will do what they want and there is no predictor." Reality sunk in, as I soon realized the pitfalls that faced me by attempting to try to change human behavior through legislative fiat. Ted went on to talk about how a Roman Senator actually murdered another Senator over a power struggle while at the same time they were trying to pass laws to keep the citizenry from doing the same. That was over 2,000 years ago! Sound familiar?

I didn't like hearing what Ted was trying to tell me. I desperately wanted to fix the problem. But I knew Ted was right as rain. Let's take a look at some of the great and successful movements across this country. MADD, Mothers Against Drunk Drivers, was founded in 1980. Still, every day in America someone is killed or maimed by an impaired or intoxicated driver. Drunk driving penalties are strengthened yearly by state legislatures in answer to this growing problem, yet according to CDC Motor Vehicle Safety Division, 28 people in the United States die daily in motor vehicle crashes that involve an alcohol-impaired driver.

The Civil Rights Movement came of age in the 1960's with Dr. Martin Luther King's leadership, yet today in America we see racism on the rise with protesters chanting *black lives matter* and professional football players refusing to stand for the national anthem in protest. *The Anti-War Movement* came of age during Vietnam War, which eventually ended in 1972 with the pullout of American forces from Saigon. Yet today in 2017, America finds herself still embroiled in war since retaliation of the 9-11 attacks on American soil in the year 2001. This fifteen-year war, started in 2002, was described by President Bush as "not your father's war." Bush was right about that. This is an observation noted by my 27-year old daughter who remarked on how her generation of millennials have known two political maxims to be true: war for fifteen years and a bad economy that has kept wages at 1980 levels. So where does this leave us? We will need more than just well-intentioned laws to cure sexual misconduct.

Another story offers a historical perspective where I had a front row seat. Oregon Senator Bob Packwood resigned from the United States Senate in 1995 under the threat of sexual harassment, abuse and assault charges from 20 women. I remember hearing about the rumors, behaviors, and actions – both good and bad. As a young Republican coming up through the ranks, I and others regarded Packwood as an icon for anyone in Oregon working to change the system or enhance their own careers. He helped with careers and reformed Oregon politically.

Packwood held powerful senate positions and was regarded as having one of the finest minds in the U.S. Senate, bar none. The citizen lobby group I worked with in the late 1980's and early 1990's sought out Packwood for help on Oregon's timber wars and other natural resource-based legislation.

During our trips to Washington, D.C., he met with us to help craft our legislative agenda. On his trips back to Oregon, we hosted luncheons and events to help him win re-election and in turn further our own causes as well. I got to know Bob Packwood. I like Bob Packwood. To this day I will always admire him for his willingness to spend time with people like myself, who at the time held no positions of importance. He had an ability to make people feel comfortable and employed great speaking ability as well. We still talk at events as I am eager to hear his take on elections or anything political.

So, it was great sadness that his resignation came at a time when Oregon needed his national influence. I remember one trip specifically where we attended a Washington, D.C. reception. It was hosted in a hotel ballroom complete with food, drinks and music. In attendance were the usual hanger-on's, lobbyists, government employees, staffers, and constituents like myself. We gathered at the appointed time, socialized and waited for his arrival, as he was late of course.

I remember when he walked into the room full of people that evening. I was standing by the door and I observed a younger man immediately hand him a glass of red wine which he downed in one drink. I was surprised by that and the additional drinks provided to him by others. He continued to drink throughout the evening. Later he stood and gave a remarkable speech without missing a beat or fact. At 29, I was mesmerized.

In retrospect, Packwood later cited his drinking as reason for his behavior. An excuse? Maybe. Alcoholism may be a contributing factor, but I doubt if it can be solely attributed for any man's sexual misbehavior. After the sexual harassment cases came to light, Packwood entered the Hazelden Foundation clinic for alcoholism in Minnesota (Trip, Gabriel 1993).

After his resignation, Ethics Committee member, Republican Senator Mitch McConnell publicly referred to Packwood's "habitual pattern of aggressive, blatantly sexual advances, mostly directed at members of his own staff or others whose livelihoods were connected in some way to his power and authority as a Senator. (Seelye, Katharine Q. 2017) While watching a local TV news cast, I distinctly remember him saying in reference to his mistreatment of women, "I just didn't get it." In Packwood as in other offenders, there remains an unhealthy attachment between his brain function, his anatomy, and the viewing of women as sexual objects.

Fast forward to today. Senator McConnell, now the Senate Majority Leader dealing with exponentially more of these cases, finds himself in a familiar position of managing a crisis that has the potential to take down America's most powerfully elite. It all could have been avoided. Sexual misconduct by members of Congress is well known, then and now. Yet little effort has been made through the years by its own members to curb the nastiness.

Looking-the-other-way behavior by men in power who don't engage in sexual misconduct yet know it exists must be regarded as complicit until they too step up to stop the abuse in one of the most powerful government institutions on the planet –- the United States Senate.

So, what is the answer? How can passing laws help?

Strengthening our laws can give a guideline for citizens to follow and implement penalties for those in power who allow it to happen. Stopping sexual mistreatment upon powerless women – or the mistreatment of any person -- needs to become a part of an attitude of public service.

First is reporting. A bad behavior can't be stopped if the right people are not made aware of it. As more women come forward exposing high-powered men of Hollywood, politics, local and state governments, and business, we can only hope this sad epidemic of behavioral corruption will end.

Second, law enforcement must act and not ignore the reports. Long gone are the days where a woman first needed to *prove* that a man assaulted her physically, verbally or emotionally before an investigation could take place.

Third, strengthening the penalties. Keeping in mind that the rules have changed, a discussion needs to take place on how far back in time perpetrators need to be held accountable. Current perpetrators need to pay with their checkbook, their time and any other items they hold dear. If the statute of limitations applies to many laws in this country, then sexual harassment, abuse and rape is no exception.

Fourth, change the behavior and identify the thought processes that go into sexual abuse. Through trainings, counseling,

and education, behavior can be relearned with willing participants. I will always maintain that sexual harassment is a behavior,
and behavior is a choice.

Fifth, end the secrecy and stop the slush fund of payouts in
hush money by congressmen who supposedly abused people. The
U.S. Congress reached a new low with the mere establishment of
the Office of Compliance. Reportedly, this fund set up by Congressional lawyers, is said to have secretly shelled out more than
$17-million in the last 20 years on workplace settlements and
awards with at least 260 claims paid out (thehill.com). The secret
payouts from the Office of Compliance fund are in direct violation
the U.S. Constitution Appropriations clause which states, "No
money shall be drawn from the Treasury, but in Consequence
of Appropriations made by Law; and a regular Statement and
Account of the Receipts and Expenditures of all public Money
shall be published from time to time, Article 1, Section 9, Clause
7" (theheritage.org). The fact that it's secret makes it illegal.

End the secret Congressional fund now. Disclose the users. I
personally would like to know how many women, if any, used this
fund to their own advantage. There is no finer example of pay-to-
play; Congress seems to have invented it.

And I leave the hardest solution for last: let's try to understand our unique and differing attitudes and approaches regarding the sexes. Relationships between the sexes can be challenging.
Teach women not only how to defend themselves, but to stay out
of the situations in the first place. Teach men that acting out their
fantasies is inappropriate, and behavior is always a choice.

Not until and unless the men, and women, understand deep
down in their psyche that their personal codes of conduct are as
important as breathing air itself, our young girls will always be
subject to these heinous acts and our young boys will be doomed

to repeat the same. We must no longer remain silent. We must speak up and report what has been done to us and support our sisters in their efforts in fighting these heinous sexual deviations against women. We must also learn to understand the inherent difference between men and women and how to get along. As women, this includes knowing that not all gestures, looks or even some comments should be construed as sexual misconduct, lest we vilify all unwanted behavior as troublesome and ultimately alter productive workplace relationships, but not for the better. As men, we must understand that just because a woman smiles and is polite, that is not an invitation for unwanted sexual advances.

As a county commissioner from Oregon's third largest county, our employees were required to attend such trainings and worked on establishing their own guidelines. We even implemented employee-written goals and programs to ensure awareness and respect to individual's behavior and rights. I'm not saying our program was an end to all abuse, but at least we are trying. At least the employees know that management initiated an effort on their behalf.

My husband, who works for a federal government agency confirms the opportunities for awareness and education are plentiful at his job as well. Yet, we still fall short on the decency scale when reducing women to sex objects. At my husband's place of employment, he says he has not seen or heard of sexual harassment of any kind, nor has he overheard men engaging in locker room talk or any other behavior derogatory toward women. It can be done. New legislation must be written – and adhered to – to fix this sexual morality crisis. The issue must be addressed in our courts and at the highest levels of law-making possible.

The Folly of Sexual Harassment Training

***

"Congress has been a breeding ground for a hostile work environment for far too long," stated Rep. Jackie Speier, Democrat member of Congress from California's 13th District. She should know. Speier tells of her own incident of sexual abuse at the hands of a superior while she was a young staffer on Capitol Hill.

Speier, along with Rep. Barbara Comstock, Republican from Northern Virginia, is leading efforts in Congress to reform Capitol Hill's workplace harassment and discrimination policies. Since the *Weinstein Effect* took root as the new term in American vocabulary to express the epidemic of sexual abuse, harassment and even rape, suddenly there seems to be an urgency to address the decade's-old issue.

Congress has historically ignored efforts by women legislators to reform its harassment trainings for itself and staffers. In 2014, Speier was the first Member to introduce a bill to combat sexual harassment in the House. The bill failed to gain attention of male dominated leadership and died. Another effort to obtain $500,000 in funding for sexual harassment training through the controversial Office of Compliance was dropped by the male dominated Senate in 2015.

Previously, Congress has had several members resign as accusations come forth of sexual harassment: Sen. Al Franken, (D, MN); Rep. John Conyers, (D, MI); Rep Trent Franks, (R, AZ); Rep. Ruben Kiheun, (D, NV); and Rep. Blake Farenhold, (R, TX). Allegedly, other members have accusations looming over their heads as Speier herself has alluded to in testimony she gave in a November, 2017 hearing. Fearful of being exposed, other male members of Congress have decided not to seek re-election.

Additionally, Assemblywoman Cristina Garcia who represents the 58th District of California, is on board in her effort to stop the abuse through legislation in her state. Garcia shared publicly that she was grabbed by a senior lobbyist, two weeks after she was sworn into office in 2012. However, that was not what upset her the most about the incident. "I was even more so upset and shocked by my peers and the senators telling me to be quiet and not to say anything.' I thought, "'If this is happening to me, what's happening to my staffers who don't have a title?'" (theelitedaily.com)

As I write this book, dozens more women legislators from California and other states have come forward in their support of changing behavior in America's most powerful governmental institutions. The issue is wide-spread as it sweeps across our country. It would seem that women have reached the end of their ropes as they report more cases of workplace sexual harassment.

Representative Nancy Pelosi, Democrat from California, former speaker of the House of Representatives in U.S. Congress and now Democrat Minority Leader, finally admitted after previously bumbling in a TV news show where she doubted the accusation of a woman who came forward accusing Rep. John

Conyers of sexual harassment. She quickly reversed her reticence upon investigating fully and stated, "No matter how great an individual's legacy is, it's not a license for harassment." It appears that Pelosi, one of the most powerful women politicians in America, was unaware of abuse by one of her own caucus members.

Conyers, a democrat elected in 1964 from Michigan, was the highest-ranking democrat on the powerful Judiciary committee and, up until accusations against him were made, enjoyed a reputation of esteem. Conyers, 88, announced his "retirement" as the longest-serving member of Congress and has denied accusations made through the woman's lawyer, although he reportedly paid her over $27,000 from his Congressional account upon her departure from his employment. Other payouts from Congressional members came through the Congress-created Office of Compliance and remain secret. Pelosi reversed her own initial analysis of Conyers' actions once she looked at the evidence brought forth. She showed shock over this incident as it occurred in her own caucus. John Conyers "retired" from Congress on December 5, 2017, after Pelosi demanded he resign his seat, along with House Speaker Paul Ryan and other Congressional members.

Senator Chuck Grassley, Republican from Iowa, agrees with Speier and is calling for the "immediate implementation of a policy requiring all new Senate employees" as well as "all current employees who have not yet received training" to go through online or in-person sexual harassment training. (vox.com) Currently, U.S. Capitol employees are not required to undergo harassment training. Grassley, now 84, penned the 1995 *Congressional Accountability Act*, which enacted civil rights, labor, workplace safety, and health laws to Congress and agencies under the legislative branch in response to then Sen. Bob Packwood's (R-OR) resignation over sexual harassment accusations.

Admittedly, many staffers who work in Congressional offices have no idea how to report sexual abuse or harassment. Rare are the opportunities for them to actually sit down with their boss for a talk - either a representative or senator - because of the busy nature of Congress's schedules. Their bosses are seldom available to them. The Members' time is split between committee assignments, writing legislation, serving the people back home, leadership caucus meetings and don't forget running for re-election which happens every two years - even constituents' visits are limited by minutes with their elected official. This is not an excuse so much as it is a harsh observation of a workplace environment where demands on a congressman's time runs high and power is brokered daily.

The opportunity to serve a member of Congress is a sought-after position by a young professional trying to establish a career, thus padding a resume. Many people apply for these positions and few are chosen. The hours are long and demanding yet rewarding with high turnover of staff. What is overlooked are the rights these workers have especially given the severe time constraints and overwhelming demands on Congressional offices. These same young, inexperienced workers are the very targets for people in high power. They have not yet developed the survival skills needed to keep the sexual assaults at bay, or the courage to say "no" out of fear of reprisal. They fear that reporting the mistreatment will result in their firing thus permanently damage their careers.

"There are two things that are really problematic," explained Harvard sociologist Frank Dobbin, commenting on the reasons behind sexual harassment. "One is when there are huge power differentials between men and women, and the other problem is when you have huge differentials in the gender composition of a job" (eeoc.gov).

House Speaker Paul Ryan (R-WI) is completely supportive in Speier's quest in making anti-harassment trainings mandatory for themselves as well as all staff. "Our goal is not only to raise awareness, but also make abundantly clear that harassment in any form has no place in this institution," Ryan said in a statement from November 2017. (vox.com) While the road to prosperity is paved with good intentions unrealized, I remain optimistic yet guarded that real reform will happen. After all, it's Congress. They voted to make harassment training mandatory on November 24, 2017. Members and staff will have to complete the training no later than 180 days after the second session of the current Congress begins in January.

As the daily deluge of high-profile sexual harassment allegations come in from Hollywood, Congress and state legislatures across America, as well as the mega media networks who report on this matter, political leaders are grasping desperately at a simple solution: make anti-sexual harassment training mandatory in their own workplace.

There's just one problem with this initiative: It's probably not going to do anything to curb sexual harassment. Experts who study workplace harassment view these trainings as more of a strategic defense against future lawsuits than a solution to a pervasive problem.

This feel-good legislation will satisfy some members of Congress who in their minds can go back to work on the real problems voters sent them to Washington to solve. No doubt the baton will be passed onto others to implement. However, a year from now it could be discovered that little success was actually made in stopping sexual harassment. Why? Because sexual harassment training doesn't work.

Elizabeth Tippett, an associate professor at the University of Oregon School of Law has studied the effectiveness of harassment trainings in her 48-page paper where she quotes 151 citations (Tippet, Elizabeth Brekley Journal of Employment & Labor Law 2018). She outlines 74 current legal and historical harassment trainings through the 1980's and 1990's. What she discovered, along with others, makes Congress's potential work on passing meaningful mandatory harassment trainings seem like an exercise in folly unless of course some real teeth are put into the bill.

She claims sexual harassment trainings used by companies are outdated and overemphasize sexual conduct at the expense of other forms of harassment. "Current trainings include large quantities of tangential legal information. They also tend to suggest that relatively trivial slights could give rise to harassment-related liability." She also claims the trainings fail to drill down to the root cause of harassment behavior. Overall, trainings tend to gloss over the discrimination-based origins and purpose of harassment law, which might otherwise serve as a moral anchor for the trainings." For many, the key here is the moral compass (or lack thereof) the individual possesses that would empower them to verbally, physically, or sexually abuse another person in the first place.

As Congress moves forward to pen legislation to make mandatory sexual harassment trainings under their own tent, they won't have to look far to find solutions or affirmation that the problem is roaring nationally The U.S. Equal Opportunity Commission, EEOC, has been busy analyzing the issue and has published their findings in a paper called Select Task Force on the Study of Harassment in the Workplace (www.eeoc.gov). This 2016 study confirms what is reported anecdotally in the news media today by women: workplace harassment remains a persistent problem with "almost fully one-third of the approximately 90,000 charges received by EEOC in fiscal year 2015 included an allegation of workplace harassment."

The second finding from the task force affirms sexual harassment goes unreported with roughly three out of four individuals who experienced harassment never even talked to a supervisor, manager, or union representative about the harassing conduct. In listening to these women, in almost every case, they say fear of losing their jobs keeps them quiet. They either silently absorb the abuse or quit their jobs.

On the bright side, if there is such hope, the task force study cites further evidence that a compelling business case exists for stopping and preventing harassment. When employers consider the costs of workplace harassment, they often focus on legal costs, and with good reason. Last year, EEOC alone recovered $164.5 million for workers alleging harassment - and these direct costs are just the tip of the iceberg. Beyond that, workplace harassment affects all workers, and its true cost includes decreased productivity, increased turnover, medical ailments and reputational harm. All of this is a negative pull on performance - and the bottom-line.

The unintended financial costs not only hit the companies, but the injured parties as well. Women also experience economic hardship as they are sometimes forced to leave their jobs to escape the terror of the continued unwanted sexual advances.

According to a 2017 study, "The Economic and Career Effects of Sexual Harassment on Working Women," (doi.org) sexual harassment's financial impact "is comparable to experiencing other negative life events: serious injury or illness, incarceration, assault—suggesting that sexual harassment may have analogous scarring effects."

The three-university study specifically keyed in on women who experienced unwanted touching or multiple harassing behaviors, and said they reported "significantly greater financial stress in the subsequent two years, establishing a clear temporal order between sexual harassment, job change, and financial stress."

The study continues to stress how unwanted, unwelcomed sexual harassment can disrupt the career path of its innocent victims and potentially leave them worse off financially. It also underscores the desperate measures that victims are forced to take to escape toxic workplaces.

Hopefully, the efforts Congress takes on legislation will not sit on the shelf as they move on to more popular policy initiatives. What Congress needs is a reporting outlet established with easy rules to follow with an impartial committee or human resource department to oversee the complaints with enough authority to act upon the complaints. It sounds easy enough. But the big question remains: will Congress police itself? Up until now, members have ignored the decades-old problem.

The easy part is passing the initial law or resolution. The hard part comes in implementing the good ideas while encouraging the members who actually voted for the trainings to take seriously the impact of their own harmful actions. The EEOC Task Force Study acknowledges the shortcomings in harassment training. It also gives dozens of remedies to help any private organization or government succeed with their education efforts to train employees. Recognizing that dedicated employees deserve to work in a harassment-free environment, finally gives these front-line employees a voice where none existed for them before.

Some male members of Congress must realize that they don't serve in a frat house: they serve in the House of Representatives. The worst offenders won't admit to having a problem until, like a child who gets caught and spanked, they suddenly become contrite. The realization sets in that voters could actually throw them out of office, or worse yet, they could be forced to resign by their own members! This is not surprising since many elected officials come from the states, the districts, and towns where they learned that "trash talking" about women or sexual harassment was a normal part of growing up. Remember the discussion on states' own lawmaking history of rape laws in the previous chapter? Many of today's male members of Congress came of age in the very system wrought with failure to actually identify and solve the problem. I doubt the sudden realization that they must change their motive of operation will alter a life time of learned behavior, especially since they find little wrong in it to begin with. They got away with it far too long. But times are changing.

Companies that truly want to stop sexual harassment have to work on closing gaps in gender equality by increasing the number of women in leadership roles, while conveying that harassment won't be tolerated. "If women were more represented at higher levels of organizations, including the very top, and represented in significant numbers, that might help," explained Lauren Edelman, a professor of law and sociology at Berkeley Law (vox.com).

Traditional methods can backfire, but ideas like teaching bystanders to intervene and promoting more women have proved effective in combatting workplace sexual harassment. Training is essential but not enough, researchers say. To actually prevent harassment, companies need to create a culture in which women are treated as equals and employees treat one another with respect.

Here are evidence-based ideas for how to create a workplace culture that rejects harassment. Researchers say they apply not just to men attacking women but to other types of harassment, too.

Empower the Bystander: This action will empower the workforce to act and become part of the solution while accepting a leadership role. Training sessions could teach employees how to recognize the behavior, approach an uncomfortable situation through humorous dialogue or to break the tension by dropping a book, or pretending to befriend the victim. Bystander Training is rare in corporate America but has been used on college campuses and in the military successfully.

Trainers suggest choices for what to do as a bystander. Most don't advise confronting the harasser in the moment, because it can escalate and put the bystander in jeopardy. If comfortable doing so, they suggest, a bystander can say something like, "That joke wasn't funny."

Encourage Civility: One problem with traditional training, researchers say, is that it teaches people what not to do, but is silent on what they should do. Civility training aims to fill that gap. New training programs put forward by the EEOC, start by asking participants to brainstorm a list of respectful behaviors. They include having conversations that include praising work, refraining from interrupting and avoiding multitasking during conversations. A big one is spotlighting contributions by people who are marginalized, according to the guidelines.

Train Seriously and Often: The most effective training, according to the American Psychological Association, is at least four hours, in person, interactive and tailored for the particular workplace. A paper was published in November of 2013 analyzing diversity training outcomes. For instance, a restaurant's training would differ from a law firm's. It's best if facilitated by the employees' supervisor or an external expert, not an H.R. official with no direct oversight (onlinelibrary.wiley.com).

Trainings should be frequent, and the topic should come up in conversations about other things, whether strategy or customer service. "We're talking about literally generations of people getting away with abusing power," clarified Robert Eckstein, lead researcher at University of New Hampshire Sociology

Department. "Thinking you can change that in a one-hour session is absurd. You're not going to just order some bagels and hope it goes away."

Promote More Women: Common sense tells us since men in supervisory positions are the likely sexual harassers in the work place, then promote more women to management. Respectful equitable relationships will follow once the power differential becomes more balanced. Much research on this issue has shown that companies that have more women in leadership have less sexual harassment.

As a raft of studies has shown, harassment flourishes in work-places where men dominate in management and women have little power. Second, harassment flourishes in organizations where few women hold the "core" jobs. As long as men dominate in manage-ment, it'll be up to them to make those changes, states Dobbin.

Encourage Reporting: Most women don't report harassment. Some don't want to take the risk alone for fear of retaliation or they don't know who to report it to. Many assume that if there are no programs in place that nothing will be done to address the problem. They may not want to end someone's career — they just want to stop the behavior and to continue to work peacefully.

Ian Ayres, a Yale professor of law and management, pub-lished a paper in 2012 entitled, "Information Escrows," about using this system for harassment reporting (digitalcommons.law.yale.edu). Victims submit a time-stamped complaint against an abuser and can request that it is reported only if another employee files a complaint against the same person. A team or designee can then assess the benefits and costs of allegation escrows and dis-cuss how they might be applied to a variety of claims, including sexual harassment, date rape, adultery, and corporate and public whistleblowing.

Researchers also suggested proportional consequences: Harassers shouldn't be automatically fired; it should depend on the offense. "If the penalty is someone's always going to get fired, lots of targets won't come forward," revealed Shannon Rawski, a professor of business at the University of Wisconsin, Oshkosh. "But research suggests if you let the small things slide, it opens the door for more severe behaviors to enter the workplace."

As Congress has already passed a bill to make harassment trainings mandatory in the House of Representatives, they along with private companies suffering from the same failure in human resource management need to remember a major point about anti-harassment trainings: in isolation, they are nothing more than a bandage solution. Congress and Companies must reckon with their cultures and address systemic inequalities within their organizations that may be enabling harassment if they truly want to prevent this type of discrimination from occurring.

Speaker Paul Ryan seems dedicated in his effort to end sexual harassment in the House of Representatives while making the body more accountable. He explained, "I think nowhere should that be more obvious and apparent than working here on Capitol Hill. So, I think here in Congress, we should set ourselves to standards that we expect of other people [to follow] and we should set high standards for ourselves so that we can be role models and set examples, and clearly people have been falling short of that and I think we always have to endeavor to do a better job on that." (npr.org)

As Congress swiftly enacted legislation in November of 2017 to solve the harassment problem, some of their own members remain guarded in their expectations for success. Both Rep. Speier and Assemblywoman Garcia will fight to hold powerful men in Congress accountable for what seems like a pandemic disease running across America. They both hope that young women are not deterred from entering into politics because of sexual harassment.

"Although we're still far from gender-equal representation in politics, change is definitely in the works to help out the next wave of women to enter the political realm," commented California's Garcia.

"It is time to throw back the curtain on the repulsive behavior that until now has thrived in the dark without consequences," said Rep. Speier as she continues on her quest with the #MeTooCongress campaign.

The Language We Use Equals the Deeds We Do

U p to this point in this book, the discussion has focused on the obvious and overt physical sexual assault, abuse and rape which is easily defined. Those horrid actions inflicted upon women are the most indefensible because of the degree to which the violence is felt.

There She Is…The Miss America Pageant, one of America's oldest scholarship competitions where beautiful women rise to the top with hopes of being crowned Miss America, came under fire when it was revealed that three of its top officials sent slanderous emails insulting its own contestants. President Josh Randle, CEO Sam Haskell and Chairman Lynn Weidner resigned under pressure in the wake of a scandal that revealed emails criticizing women over their appearances and intelligence. Haskell remains the main target of the ongoing investigation. Haskell sent emails calling contestants "cunts and malcontents" while referring to their ill-shaped bodies. A series of emails purportedly written in 2014 and 2015 and shared between Haskell and other organization leaders, referred to former Miss America contestants with offensive slang terms for a female body part and joked about another winner's death.

Former Fox News anchor Gretchen Carlson will serve as the new chair of Miss America's board of directors, becoming the first former pageant winner to lead the organization. In 2016, Carlson settled a sexual harassment lawsuit with 21st Century Fox against former Fox News CEO Roger Ailes for $20 million. Disgraced former CEO Haskell appeared to dislike Gretchen Carlson, who won the Miss America title in 1989 and was on the organization's board of directors for many years. The root cause of their disdain, according to multiple sources, was Carlson's push to modernize the organization with reforms like eliminating the swim suit competition, and her refusal to attack former Miss Americas. Former Miss America winners Laura Kaeppeler Fleiss, Heather French Henry and Kate Shindle will join Carlson on the board as they clean up the corruption. It would appear that Karma won the day on this shift in management personnel as bad language fell the leadership on one of America's oldest associations.

But let's consider the more hidden forms of sexism, which I believe are more prevalent in their influence in our workplaces and in our play-places and are most always ignored. For lack of a better term, I'll call it *locker room talk*. Before he decided to run for office, President Trump used this moniker to describe in his famous faux pas caught on tape with Billy Bush when bragging about his sexual proclivities with women. Trump wasn't the only person to label vulgar sex talk as *locker room banter*.

For the purest at heart, according to Webster's, the term dates back to 1921 and is defined as "relating to, or suitable for use in a locker room; especially of a coarse or sexual nature."

This type of talk objectifies women for sexual purposes and reflects some men's attitudes regarding sexism. In order for sexual abuse, assault or harassment to occur, one must first think about the action. Thinking comes before talking which I believe is the precursor to actions of rape, abuse, assault and harassment. In other words, for an action to take place, one must first think about it, the second step is talking, then finally, the act is carried out: think, talk, act. It's just not enough to cease sexually harassing women physically, the attitudes and thinking must also change – or the bar is set way too low for real behavioral change.

Gone should be the days when it's acceptable for grown men to revert back to the boys' mentality, huddled together in their closed groups like a football team ready to call its secret play. Huddles used to occur around the office water cooler back when water coolers still existed. Now huddles just happen anywhere. They laugh, cajole and carry on in conversations with their cohorts espousing derogatory comments toward women.

Here's one example of a real life happening that might have been construed as *locker room talk*. During my legislative days in 2003, I observed such behavior in the hallways where the confines of our legislative offices kept us all in close contact. A small group of my colleagues assembled themselves in a little huddle and began to talk, laugh and share what appeared to be having an overall good time. This activity, absence of a woman's presence, happened enough times over the ensuing weeks that it made me take notice. Thinking they were discussing some important policy decision or action that I should know about, one day I boldly walked over to the group of men and asked, "What's up?" It was a natural move for me since I was voted, by them, into a leadership position within our own caucus.

Obviously I felt comfortable enough to approach them since I considered these men friends. Upon my arrival, the men immediately stopped talking and looked at me. I felt uncomfortable as if I had violated some fraternity code that beaconed "no women allowed." But remember, this was the very public hallways of the Oregon State Legislature where people of all types were conducting business. The conversations should not have been that closed or private. My fellow legislators quickly disbanded, returning to their offices as if my presence would give them a communicable disease.

Their actions could have been taken two different ways. One -- as their leader, friend and someone they respected -- they might have felt like I was a mother figure and they had gotten caught having a good time by not working. Of course, that was not my intent. The second scenario, which I was later lead to believe was the most likely, was that these normally good men got caught trash-talking women.

Look, fellas, if you can't reveal your conversation in mixed company, shut it down! It's obviously inappropriate and does not belong at work. Furthermore, if your conversations are innocent, then conduct them in such a manner that they can't be construed as offensive. If men don't hold each other accountable or take responsibility then what's at risk are your reputations, trust and the ultimate cooperation you all seek for healthy relationships and ultimately success in your endeavors. It's just like scolding a four-year-old for stealing his sister's toy. The situation becomes a teachable moment. It's your teachable moment.

All this seemed innocent enough if it hadn't left me scratching my head over their reluctance to continue the conversation in my presence. Was it *locker room talk?* Several other times, I attempted to enter into their world of group talk again only to be treated with the same cold shoulder. Today in 2018, I still remember the feeling of segregation and wonder...what were they saying that couldn't be shared? In light of the sensitivity to anything regarding the treatment of women, men should take care and guard themselves against being misconstrued or mis-understood. Exclusionary conversations in a public forum are impolite at the very least.

A male perspective is offered up by psychologist Shaun R. Harper, Ph.D. "Unfortunately, the kinds of words we heard from Trump are commonly spoken when men are with other men. Those who participate in this "banter" are rewarded. Those who choose not to engage, and especially guys who critique such state-ments, have their masculinities questioned and risk being placed on the outskirts of social acceptance."

Harper, professor and executive director of the Race and Equity Center at the University of Southern California and President of the Association for the Study of Higher Education, revealed that he knows from his research that confronting peers is difficult. He also counsels hundreds of high school and college age young men (washingtonpost.com).

"Rarely does one man hold another accountable or raise his consciousness about the vile acts he's describing. When men fail to challenge other men on troubling things they say about and do to women, we contribute to cultures that excuse sexual harassment, assault and other forms of gender violence," explained Harper.

At the very least these types of conversations ultimately result in exclusionary treatment. This reflects some men's attitudes towards women's presence in the workplace and could be con-sidered workplace discrimination. I have good company in shar-ing this opinion: The United States Supreme Court stated in the landmark case of *Meritor Savings Bank v. Vinson* in 1986, that workplace harassment was an actionable form of discrimination prohibited by Title VII of the Civil Rights Act of 1964. The court further states "by proving that discrimination based on sex has created a hostile or abusive work environment." Closed group conversations that are overheard by others based on women's sexuality most definitely would be defined as a hostile workplace environment. In light of the very public accusation where we see very powerful rich men fall, it's only logical that conversations based upon the sexualization of women will have no tolerance in the workplace.

Top managers and human resource professionals are becoming more sensitive to this type of chatter in their workplace for many reasons. It just doesn't make for a happy workplace environment. When people are happy they are productive. When productivity increases so does the bottom line. Good managers know that when people are happy they will tend to overlook smaller indiscretions that will in turn keep complaints and lawsuits out of the human resources office.

One study goes as far to say that a *look* or *gossip* is considered a form of sexual harassment. This strict technical definition can cut both ways and this author remains guarded and not in total agreement as to the degree to which such conversations should be measured. With that in mind, these researchers defined sexual harassment in seven different ways: 1. unwanted touching; 2. offensive jokes, remarks, or gossip directed at the study subject; 3. offensive jokes, remarks, or gossip about others; 4. direct questioning about a subject's private life; 5. staring or invasion of a subject's personal space; 6. staring or leering at a subject in a way that made her uncomfortable; and 7. pictures, posters or other materials that the subject found offensive (McLaughlin, Heather, Uggen, Christopher, Blackstone, Amy 2017).

Now that is a big tent of behavior to consider. It would be almost impossible to find a work place in America that is sanitized to the degree as the previous definition suggests and why would we want it.

I predict as the pendulum swings to the side of *zero tolerance* for any conversation based upon the differences of men and women, that healthy workplace relationships could become stifled and unproductive, lacking the good energy we humans need to feel worthy. Fear of messing up is a big predictor of behavior. Do we women want that? No, of course not. But what we do want is for the crap to stop and for the good men to step up and help where women can't.

Dr. Harper affirms that men's leadership is much needed to curb workplace sexism. He feels it's his duty to show men how hurtful *locker room talk* can be. "I share some responsibility for rape, marital infidelity and other awful things that men do. I want other men to recognize this, too — not only because they have mothers, wives, sisters, aunts or daughters – but because sexism hurts all women and men in our society" (washingtonpost.com). Thank you, Dr. Harper.

Most likely a manager or boss is unable to distinguish if the verbal exchanges at the huddle is *locker room talk* or is a symptom of a greater workplace behavioral problem. Obviously, not all men participate in this type of talk and for those who don't, we need your leadership.

What I'm saying is this: men, help yourselves and help us to create more peaceful and dynamic workplace environment.

Let us all remember; we are not living in an abyss of them versus us: quite the contrary. Smart people will recognize that if it's bad for women, it will ultimately prove to be bad for men. However, if it's good for women, then it's good for men. Dr. Phil's famous statement comes to mind, "If mama ain't happy, nobody's happy." Truer words were never spoken.

Television personality, Megyn Kelly, who as a former Fox anchor announced she was sexually assaulted by billionaire Fox

News CEO Roger Ailes, wrote in her online blog, "Perhaps the most critical solution lies in partnership with the men. The harassers must stop; we know this. But male titans of industry must stand up for decency." (Kelly, Megyn 2017) I agree with this statement as we move forward to identify the culprits, its origins and in turn stop the behavior that causes the abuse, mistreatment and assault of women.

As in the Harvey Weinstein case, his hand-picked, billionaire board members for The Weinstein Company (TWC) couldn't fly the coop fast enough in their actions to flee 'ole Harvey and company once sexual misconduct charges gained national attention. This all-male group of billionaire board members (I call them BBMs) lacked real leadership when it was needed the most. Instead of staying with the company to heal its reputation, they scampered in the opposite direction like rain-soaked cats seeking dry shelter. Why would these once loyal "friends" leave so quickly? To protect themselves of course. They obviously had little interest in helping the victims or in cleaning up the Harvey-imposed sexual abuse scandal from the company they once so proudly served. Why? Maybe they didn't know what to do? Or they feared for repercussions at their own companies they spent a lifetime building.

They soon realized their own reputations were jeopardized and collectively billions -- if not trillions -- of dollars from their own companies could be risked. It would leave some watchers to wonder that *if* these BBM's allowed this to happen under their TWC watch, what were they doing at their own companies? Currently all have refused attempts by news media to comment on events that led up to their departure. It would appear that these BBM's chose silence coupled with complicity to save themselves. Let the victims be damned.

While serving on the board of TWC, the BBM's didn't get to be billionaires from lack of courage or being stupid. Quite the opposite. They were chosen by Harvey, et al, to serve because of their acquired wealth and position. Missing from their current behavior is the past innate courage and smarts these guys used to make their own successes.

Could it simply be that these BBM's realized they didn't belong in this type of philosophical den of deceit and couldn't leave fast enough? Research evidence supports their actions. According to Christopher Freiman, assistant professor of philosophy at the College of William and Mary in Williamsburg, Virginia, men see the problem with speaking about women negatively as wrong yet many remain silent. Why don't they speak up? Freiman suggests that in these kinds of situations, we are thwarted by our need to belong. "We don't want to appear arrogant, untoward or rude… So, we swallow our objections instead of speaking up. Our desire to be accepted overwhelms our commitment to moral decency. We "go along to get along," and "in defiance of what we really value or believe because we don't want any trouble." (psychology-today.com) Could it really be that simple? Men lack courage.

According to psychologists Roy Baumeister and Mark Leary, the need to belong is "a powerful, fundamental, and extremely pervasive motivation." In fact, Baumeister and Leary contend that much of human behavior and even many of our thoughts and emotions are caused by the fundamental need to belong (Baumeister R.F., & Leary M.R. 1995).

Functional MRI research supports the thesis, and there appears to be a neurological basis for this. Stanford Neuroscientist David Eagleman's studies on brain science indicate that "our brains are wired to be more empathetic to those in our "in-group" than to those in the "out-group." Eagleman's F-MRI research found that "we register more empathetic pain when pain is inflicted on people we identify as being like us, even if we don't consciously think we feel differently about them." (psychologytoday.com) So if this theory is to be believed the next logical conclusion is although Weinstein's behavior is barbaric and illegal, it was part of the in-group, and therefore acceptable. The very wrong behavior of victimization and sexualization of women was considered to be part of the out-group and therefore was not worth saving.

In their defense the BBM's could claim lack of knowledge of the incidents. Okay, ignorance is accepted, just one time. Let's say that's true. Still, these are the richest, supposedly smartest men in America today. As society's most privileged, they don't get a pass. If not them, who? If not now, when?

How many BBM's exist in America today that have the power to change this sick epidemic of sexual misconduct at the corporate level, but choose to ignore it? I can't count that high.

Another category is unwanted sexual attention: actions like touching, making comments about someone's body and asking colleagues on dates after they've said no. About ten percent of men reported such behavior. Least common is sexual coercion, which includes pressuring people into sexual acts by offering rewards or threatening retaliation. Two percent of men said they had done such a thing recently. The survey suggests that, at a minimum, one in 25 men in the average American workplace identifies himself as a harasser. Also, an additional two in 25 said they did not know whether their actions could be classified in this way.

"In general, frequency is the most important component," said Louise Fitzgerald, a leading researcher on sexual harassment, who for the past 30 years has advised on the issue for the Equal Employment Opportunity Commission, the Department of Defense and the Department of Justice. "Even milder forms of harassment can be extremely damaging if they happen frequently and continue over time."

A major difference between those who harass and those who don't is the culture at their workplace. Behaviors associated with harassment are especially prevalent among men who say their company does not have guidelines against harassment, hotlines to report it or punishment for perpetrators, or who say their managers don't care, concludes the survey.

To think that the eruption of sexual abuse reports is only a female problem is short-sighted. It also has the potential to doom productive relationships that are so desperately needed in the work force, and thus increase lawsuits and cause good companies to suffer in their reputations. After all it's the unwanted male behavior toward women that's at issue. It's going to have to be men, real men, in leadership positions who stand up as examples. Women can't fight this battle alone, as one man attests to in the following observations.

The language we use also could be at fault without any of us as so much giving a second thought as to how we communicate – women included. It is ironic that as we discuss this national pandemic of sexual misconduct that has captured our attention -- that while social scientists, psychologists, doctors, leaders, and jurists struggle with defining and curing the problem -- that one single filmmaker would offer such a focused approach that we all can use.

Jackson Katz is a filmmaker, activist and educator with a small following but offers up a simple solution in the way we verbalize. "We talk about women being raped, not men raping women. We talk about women being harassed; not about how many men are harassing women. We talk about how many teenage girls got pregnant, rather than how many boys and men impregnated teenage girls," said Jackson in his *Mentors in Violence Prevention* program (Katz, Jackson MVP Mentors speech 2017).

He further points out that this passive language absolves men of all responsibility. "Even the term, "violence against women" is problematic," he proclaimed.

I, too, am guilty of merely repeating what I heard someone say. This insight is remarkable given the national conversation we're having on the sexual mistreatment of women – 'er…. should I have instead been saying, "men sexually mistreating women." We have a long way to go, me included.

When you look at the term "violence against women" nobody is doing it to them. It just happens to them, and men aren't even a part of it, comments Katz. "We need to get more men who are in business and political cultural leadership to take this stuff seriously and take it to the next level."

"Women's leadership has been incredible and transformative, but the missing piece is men's leadership," concludes Katz. Not committing sexual assault or harassment is way too low a bar for what it takes to be a good guy. These incredible comments by Katz are a plea that I hope more men will listen to.

Catholic Priest Sex Scandal

The pedophile catholic priest sex conundrum cannot be defined as ordinary workplace sexual harassment. However, the payment of lawsuits brought forth by the church laity (not an ordained minister or priest, but ordinary parishioners who play a role in the church service) as victims can certainly be classified as pay-to-play. Local archdioceses across the country continue to pay large sums of money supplied by the Sunday offering plates through lawsuits as the guilty priest is moved on to another location, rarely punished and only retired once he's too old to continue ordinary pastoral duties.

The inclusion of *The Church Scandal* for this book is relative in understanding the difficulties surrounding human behavior and the challenges facing society in curing abhorrent sexual behavior. If for no other reason, the Church has drawn us a road map to follow. We can decide to blindly follow that path, or we can decide to redraw the boundary lines.

As a practicing Catholic, I remain conflicted as I write this chapter and choosing to talk about the Catholic Church over any other church such as the Mormon Church (Latter Day Saints), Seventh-day Adventist Church, Adventist, Methodist, Evangelical, Lutheran, Fundamentalist, Pentecostal, Mennonite, Jehovah's Witnesses,

Conservative Baptist, Presbyterian or any other religious institution -who by the way are equally as guilty - is a natural as I witnessed the happenings both from the political and worship standpoints. Many people like me remain disgusted by the prospects that the Catholic Church has closed ranks and continues to harbor guilty priests now in 2018, almost two decades after the sex scandal made headlines in American newspapers. As a Christian, trying to reconcile that both good and evil exists in the same worship institution becomes problematic. It bodes several questions: Are we all just a bunch of sanctimonious hypocrites? Or should we stand arm in arm determined to stop the problem within our own ranks?

Does accepting the soundness of church doctrine in essence condone sexual pedophilia? Hopefully not, but that age-old question won't be answered on these pages as I leave that for the spiritual intellectuals to consider. What propels me, however, is to shine an even brighter light on the Catholic Church sex scandal, hoping that doing so will somehow keep the faithful vigilant in their awareness of the problem. My belief that we could be saved by a Higher Power beyond what is visibly obvious on a regular basis is a challenge for me even on good days.

Initially, my generation was aghast that God's devoted priests could perform such heinous acts on our innocent children. Parents willingly sent their children to slaughter thinking that serving communion during Sunday Mass was preparing their youth for holy adulthood, but shockingly found out years later that was not the case. One by one, victims came forward reporting the dirty deeds performed on them as children behind closed doors by these priests who were charged with educating the masses while promoting church doctrine.

Grown men continued to come forward to recount the perverted acts committed against them as children, now demanding restitution through their attorneys. As children, they were coerced and threatened into silence not to reveal the sex acts performed on them while at the same time being convinced that service to the church was a righteous pursuit lest they be sent directly to hell. Some victims were even forced as children to sign agreements ensuring their silence. Ashamed and guilt ridden these boys held the secret within their tortured psyche until at last, one brave soul after another came forward and filed public lawsuits.

The effects of carrying sexual abuse inflicted on these adult men as boys has shaken the church to its foundation as one by one they testified in depositions and court proceedings. The church scurried to stay out of headlines through legal maneuvers as many lawsuits failed to reach public court levels as settlements of undisclosed amounts of money were paid to the victims. Many faithful parishioners not wanting to believe that their beloved priest could do such a horror went as far as to blame greedy lawyers who brought the lawsuits against the archdiocese for the scandal. For too long, faithful church goers looked the other way as priests ruled supremely within the church structure. For centuries priests held influence and the ultimate power of educating and entrusting people's deepest secrets through the confessional, private counseling sessions and preaching moral imperatives through the weekly homily.

While the following story did not happen within the confines of the Catholic Church, it is a great example of how pedophiles, including priestly ones, groom their young victims:

Pedophiles Groom Their Potential Victims

I am a public-school teacher with almost 20 years classroom experience. The last statistic I knew was that 1 in 4 children have been sexually abused in some manner. If you have a classroom of 32 students, that means you statistically have 8 students who have been violated.

I have been trained to spot signs and symptoms of sexual and other abuse. Several times I have had to call Child Protective Services to report abuse. Once I even had to barricade myself and a student in my classroom until the police arrived after her crazy uncle found out she told me he was raping her on a daily basis. She was 11 years old.

I am also a mom of three daughters. My husband and I have been training them at a very early age to be aware of predators. We thought we had provided enough protection and information to keep them safe. I was wrong - sort of.

Our 12-year-old daughter decided she wanted to get her second-degree black belt. She had taken a year off and required personal lessons to get back up to speed. She is the kind of kid that is hard on herself and expects a lot. She requested that I not come in to watch the private lessons and asked if I could wait in the car and watch from the window outside? I thought that was reasonable. I was able to see the two of them- most of the time and I was only about 20 feet away. AND this "master" knew I was there watching.

To make a long story short, he started out slowly. As they were working on forms, he would "accidentally" brush up against her breast. He seemed to do that a bit more often with time. My daughter questioned if she was imagining this. One day, she was wearing a black tank top under her uniform and he asked her if that was her bra strap. She was offended and surprised, but still did not say anything to me at the time.

He graduated to larger grooming tactics. He once pressed his body tightly against hers. It bothered her, but he was a taekwondo master and owner of the studio. In her 12-year old mind, she thought he would never do anything inappropriate. It must have been a mistake. This was her teacher. After all, respect is everything in martial arts. He had elevated status in her mind's eye.

One day, they were doing floor work, and I was still sitting in my car watching, but for those few minutes I could not see them. That is when this pedophile took his test to the next level. They were doing sit ups and planks. He said to her that she was not using her core muscles. She said that she was. He put his hand on her lower abdomen to "check to see if her muscles were tightened." He then said they were not and she should put her hand on his abdomen, so she could feel what it was like. She said no and that is when he grabbed her hand and put it on his penis. At that moment, she ran out of the studio into the car and yelled at me to leave.

It was at this point that she told me everything. She told me she thought she was going crazy with all of his "sleight of hand moves." She told me it did not make sense because he was married, professed to being a "good Christian," had three kids, and was involved in the martial arts community. She thought she was imagining these things over the past three months. She was very concerned about making false accusations. She did not want to hurt him. But with this last effort he crossed the line and she knew it.

We had a long discussion about what had been going on and she said she wanted to confront him. I remembered thinking, "Woah. My 12-year-old daughter wants to confront this pedophile? Is this a good idea?" She was so angry that he would do this to her. Her rage towards him was intense. She was not going to put up with this. I told her that I would consider her approaching him but only on the condition that we role play possible scenarios of what he might say. I did this to condition her, to help her toughen up a bit, to have her think ahead so she could remain in control of the conversation and her emotions. This would be hard for any adult and she was just a kid.

I requested a meeting with him. He was such an arrogant pedophile that he truly did not know why I asked for this meeting. Did he not remember that he grabbed her hand and put it on his hard penis? How does someone forget something like that? On the day of the meeting, the three of us sat down. She let him have it. When she was done, she looked at me and asked to go to the car. I gave her my keys and she went to the car where she broke down and cried. She never let it show in front of him. I continued the conversation. I told him that I wanted ALL of my money back from the private lessons RIGHT NOW. His hands were shaking, but he opened a safe and counted out all the dollars and I got my money back. He then went on to tell me that my daughter was crazy, that she was a liar, she was simply looking for attention. I looked at him and said, "Really?" That is all it took. This is when he dropped the ball. He started telling me he did not understand girls this age. He had another student accuse him of the same thing a year ago. He also told me his sister forbids him to see his nieces and how much he missed them. WOW! I was stunned.

Once we were done, I called the police and we filed a report. The police said there was nothing that they could do but if anyone else ever complains about him or the studio, they now have a file on him. They also told my daughter that they were proud of her for telling her parents what was happening, they had never had a victim approach a predator like that and they were amazed at what a strong person she is. They thanked her because if he ever tries anything with another child again, they can go after him because he has a pattern that they have identified.

Most importantly, I helped my daughter to keep her power.

~A Mom in California

Ironically, it was the Catholic Church's own tightly knit cabal that betrayed their closely held secrets. Locally, my friend Kelly Clark, a Portland attorney of the firm O'Donnell, Clark and Crew, was the first to come forward with victims in lawsuits against the Portland, Oregon, Catholic Archdioceses. In Clark's many writings and conversations, he reiterated how the church knew of the abuse as evidenced by their own records where over the decades the accusations were filed quietly away in the church's own sealed vaults.

I first got to know Kelly while I served in the Oregon State Legislature in 2001 and was introduced to him through a mutual friend. As a former legislator, Kelly gave talks on public service, which I attended and years later I was able to engage his services for family and as a county commissioner for government.

Clark started his advocacy work on child abuse as an Oregon State legislator serving in the Oregon House from 1989 to 1993. He continued his work returning to private practice and winning a national recognized court case against the Archdiocese of Portland in the Oregon Supreme Court for the case of *Fearing v. Bucher*. That case paved the way for abuse claims that pushed the Archdiocese of Portland to seek help from the Bankruptcy Court to resolve the hundreds of claims eventually filed against it – the first Archdiocese in the country to do so. Part of the bankruptcy plan required the Portland Archdiocese to publicly release thousands of pages of secret records on Oregon priests credibly accused of child molestation.

In 2008, he won another Oregon Supreme Court case against a local police agency operating a Boy Scouts of America Explorer Post that was significant for its elimination of special immunities in the law for governmental child abusers and their employers. In September of 2012, Kelly again argued to the Oregon Supreme Court that Oregon laws giving special protection to public school teachers in cases of child abuse should be struck down as unconstitutional. Recognized by his peers locally and nationally for his expertise in this area, he wrote and spoke widely on child abuse topics for professional audiences. (crewjanci.com) Clark's advocacy work on behalf of victims has provided the road map for others to pursue legal action against some of America's most powerful institutions.

"Cover up and shut up" ruled the day until Clark and Company was able to blow the lid off and for many years he was not a popular person. As distasteful as this work was viewed by some, the public outing was the necessary evil that changed people's view of the Church as a holy sacrosanct. The good priests even went so far as to change their behavior assuring that all doors remained open during the robing of their altar servers and preparation of Sunday's communion before Mass. Additionally, the more informal education classes are held publicly with laity supervision.

In retrospect, the priest sex scandal that rocked the Christian faithful was only the start of a very public and ugly epidemic that revealed sick psychopathic behavior we didn't see coming. The groups that Clark, et al, sued – the Catholic Church, The Boy Scouts of America, and public-school districts -- paid dearly for their playing. pay-to-play lives, it would seem.

A closer look into the Catholic Church is necessary in order to understand how deep sexual abuse exists in American society and ultimately worldwide. Other religious denominations as well bear their share of the blame and are equally responsible regarding the sexual harassment and abuse front.

The Boston Archdiocese is a perfect example of how good men get caught up in scandal. Often as is the case, it's the cover up of scandal that brings down institutions and leaders. Cardinal Bernard Law, who just recently died in Rome in December 2017 at 86, enjoyed great success first as a priest then as Boston's Archbishop while becoming the Vatican's favorite American. He rose quickly through Catholic ranks as a Harvard undergraduate and attended premiere theology seminary colleges; he also had a keen intellect and an ability to communicate with the media that endeared himself to the parishioners he served. Cardinal Law was never accused of sexual abuse and personally found it horrid. However, he failed to remove, retire or defrock sexually abusive priests from the ministry over which he was in charge which ultimately culminated in his fall from grace when he retired in 2002.

The Boston attorney general's office said the abuse extended over six decades and involved at least 237 priests and 789 children; of those, 48 priests and other archdiocesan employees were alleged to have abused children while Law was leader of the Boston archdiocese. The Boston Archdiocese agreed to pay $85 million to 552 victims of clergy sex abuse in 2003 (blostonglobe.com).

Instead of defrocking the priests and firing employees, Archbishop Law simply transferred them from one unsuspecting parish to another as complaints followed. Law even put these perverted men into counseling thinking psychology could reverse or cure what God couldn't.

During the 1990's when the Catholic priest sex scandals first became public, the Catholic Church was ill-equipped to handle it from a human resource management point of view. It appeared they just didn't know what to do. Or did they just choose to ignore the problem? What the public and faithful parishioners regarded as scandalous in our modern era; the Church seemingly condoned as a way to keep its hierarchy intact. It seems that the Vatican was well aware of the sexual indiscretions of its priests and while most God-fearing laypeople prayed the behavior was an aberration, the Church secretly knew otherwise.

However, what has become so horridly insidious is that the Catholic Church chose to do little to curb the problem. Could it be that priestly sex with boys is more the norm hidden in the underbelly of church aside from what doctrine teaches the masses regarding marriage, abstinence, monogamy and the rearing of families? Ultimately, what the Church took issue with, is not so much sex abuse -- based upon their own inactions and reluctance to defrock the bad priests –- as it did with the payouts that drained the treasury, bankrupting many American archdiocese as its faithful church goers slowed their donations into the Sunday offering plate.

Truth be known, the pedophilia sex scandal that bankrupted many catholic archdioceses across America is an endemic part of a system that has occurred for a millennial. In fact, the Catholic Church has a 2,000-year history of sex abuse. In their acclaimed book, *Sex, Priests and Secret Codes*, (2006), Father Thomas Doyle, with former monks Richard Sipes and Patrick Wall, used the Church's own documents to confirm its 2,000-year problem with clerical sex abuse (alternet.org).

Father Thomas Doyle, then a canonical lawyer at the Vatican's Washington embassy, was tasked with investigating child abuse cases in the U.S. in the mid-1980s, preparing a 40-page report for the nuncio, or papal ambassador, which he said was handed to the Pope. Doyle was one of the first American priests to have broken ranks on child abuse and has stated that the Catholic Church still fails to comprehend the depth of spiritual damage done to victims (theguardian.com).

Doyle and his colleagues formed the Royal Commission in Australia at the request of the Vatican to address the problem. However, once this group of priests and monks issued a report that revealed problems for the Church, the Holy See quickly discounted the findings claiming reforms were already employed to stop the abuse (snapnet.org).

The December 16, 2017 Royal Commission's report stated covering up abuse to save the reputation of a church or school is no longer tolerable. "Bishops will be quick to scoff that the report is anti-Catholic and an attack on the tenets of faith. That is not true. The report is an attack on bad conduct, bad conduct must stop. The way to stop bad conduct is through strict adherence to good policy. It also requires that the laity, whose children have been so deeply hurt, become stakeholders in the decision-making." Additional credence is given to the church's lack of surprise over the sexual abuse problem. The Royal Commission recommended 189 reforms for Australia as it identified over 4,400 current sexually abusive priests in its 2017 report (cnn.com).

In her article, "What's Really Behind the Catholic Church's Sexual Abuse Problem?" author Harriet Fraad, methodically analyzes what many of us suspected to be the cause of pedophilia within the Catholic Church (alternet.org).

Let's start with the centuries'-old seminarian practice of the indoctrination of young men through education. Priests enter seminary before fully understanding or exploring their own sexual maturation process. Because of the celibacy requirement of priests, they grow up sexually repressed. Couple this with living in all-male domicile where females are absent, which focuses their desires upon the only outlet available – men. The vow of celibacy, prevented them from maturing emotionally, sexually and psychologically.

Therein lies the first problem: once a man dedicates himself to the priesthood, supposedly all sexual desire disappears in favor of devotion to God. Fraad believes this *learning* accounts for the pedophilia abuse of children once a priest is given control over a congregation. Many people have called for a change in Vatican policy to allow priests to marry.

Second, the lack of women beyond the traditional nunnery in convents within power structure of the Catholic Church adds to abuse. As shown in this book, institutions controlled primarily by men have a higher incidence of sexual harassment and abuse. The Catholic Church is no exception. The answer? Ordain women as priests. Remarkably, women are willing to serve within the church beyond traditional roles and have called for the Catholic Church to ordain women as clergy comparing the efforts to Jewish and Protestant denominations. (iupui.org) The Vatican has refused to consider the request even after the election of Pope Francis in 2013, who at the time was regarded liberal in many of his viewpoints.

Third, the Catholic Church's own devotion to Canon Law gave church authorities ways around from abiding by America's own form of jurisprudence. Canon Law is a complicated system of principles enforced by Catholic authorities to govern itself in all legal matters aside from any countries' jurisdiction where a particular church may reside.

New Vatican guidelines call for reporting of the abuse to local law enforcement authorities. The Vatican has always given precedence to Church Law, called Canon Law, over local criminal law in dealing with ecclesiastical crime. It does not easily tolerate interference by civil authorities in ecclesiastical matters, said David Willey a BBC News, Rome correspondent (bbc.com).

Historically, the Catholic Church has taught us well in the art of self-preservation. It survived Martin Luther's reformation in 1517 (an Augustinian monk and university lecturer in Wittenberg who protested the Pope's sale of reprieves from penance, or indulgences); the murders of the Knights Templar in 1139 (a Catholic military order), and its disappearance of untold riches; and Henry VIII expelling the Church from England in 1534 for not allowing the divorce from one his wives. If anything, the Holy See (the ecclesiastical jurisdiction of the Catholic Church in Rome) has mastered the art of survival longer than America herself has been a nation and a little ole sex scandal in the U.S. is viewed as another blimp in history that it too shall pass.

Despite the ugliness of the church's sex scandal, Catholicism seems to be as popular as ever and even increasing in some continents such as Africa. Growth numbers in the United States appear to remain static, not declining despite the sex scandal, according to World Religion News March 2016 article entitled, "Is the Catholic Church Experiencing Exponential Growth or Declining?" There are 70,412,021 registered Catholics in the United States (22% of the U.S. population), according to the American bishops' count in their Official 2016 Catholic Directory (worldreligionnew.com).

While this statistic may be considered as alarming to outsiders, could it be that people believe that once a travesty is publicly exposed, and payouts made to victims, that it won't happen again, and is therefore systematically fixed? Or do Catholics remain poised to accept the dogma that says: with adherence to Christian salvation and doctrine through faith and worship the problem will eradicate itself? Once the headlines of lawsuits die down its assumed by many that the problem no longer exists, forgiveness is given, and worship continues at its churches. But does it? What has the church really done to ensure priests no longer sexually abuse our children?

Let's use the Ford Motor Company as an example, which I believe is not an isolated view regarding human behavior. Ford Motor is once again making news headlines for all the wrong reasons. Previously, the company paid out $22 million in 1990's in damages for sexual harassment against blue collar working women at two of its Chicago factories. However, a December 2017 article in the *New York Times* reveals sexual harassment continues to be as widespread today as it was then with a new round of complaints and lawsuits being filed as a new workforce is employed. Ford officials say they view the harassment as episodic, not systemic, with an outbreak in the '90s and another beginning in 2010 as new workers were hired. A responsible citizenry should not be lulled into thinking that just because 1. the problem was exposed, and 2. lawsuits were paid -- that those two actions alone necessarily equate to fixing the problem of sexual harassment, abuse and even rape in our society.

In order to understand the complexities that surround curing the sexual abuse crisis within the Catholic Church or any other large powerful religious dynasty, one must study its structure. The Catholic Church is governed by an independent sovereign entity established through international treaty known as the *Holy See*, which is headed by the Pope. The Pope is widely considered as the only remaining absolute monarch in Europe. Within the ruling realm of the *Holy See* is Vatican City, a 110-acre city-state located in Rome, Italy. The governing body is further complicated by the establishment of legislative committees within the Vatican that adheres strictly to Canon Law, and therefore are not subject to civil law of the people or even world tribunals. World governments including the United States have historically been reluctant to challenge the authority of the Catholic Church citing the difficulties of Canon Law versus Civil Law and each country's own laws regarding the separation of religious powers. However, the United Nations has not remained silent on the issue of child sexual abuse within the Catholic Church worldwide.

Vatican watchers estimate its wealth somewhere around $10 to $15 billion, with cash flow between $100 and $150 million annually. However, the real value is difficult to track as the art collection alone is estimated to be $400 billion to $2 trillion, although it would never be sold. The Church's worldly wealth is always subject to speculation as there is no official reporting system or governing tax agency. Some speculate by protecting its priests it also protects the hierarchal power within the Vatican walls. The bishops, archbishops and cardinals all have a stake in seeing that accusations don't include them. Therefore, by failing to fully acknowledge the problem of sexual abuse, it in turn protects its priests and keeps accusers at arm's length from tainting the institution that has carefully been built since the birth of Jesus Christ.

The institutional structure of the Church, as the official entity for Catholics to achieve salvation, had become sacrosanct, Doyle wrote in his book, *Sex, Priests and Secret Codes.*

"The protection of the *institutional church* had become of all-encompassing importance to the Catholic hierarchy. The privileged status of priests in the community, he said, put them on a pedestal and in positions of power and trust. He said that could be used to control and scare victims. In the eyes of children, the priest represented God." Despite the scandal it would appear that Catholics remain as faithful as ever based on membership numbers alone. It, therefore, becomes the responsibility of the laity more than ever to ensure safety of their children and implement policies to be followed.

So, curing the problem of sexual abuse within the Catholic Church not only lies with the hierarchy itself but must come from the influence of the world community. The United Nation's Committee on the Rights of the Child (CRC) said the Vatican should "immediately remove" all clergy who are known or suspected child abusers. Clearly, the Vatican has not removed their abusive priests based upon the Royal Commission report.

In a strongly worded 2014 report, the U.N. lambasted The Holy See's "practice of offenders' mobility", referring to the transfer of child abusers from parish to parish within countries, and sometimes abroad. The U.N. report complained that the *Holy See* had not acknowledged the extent of crimes committed and had not taken the measures necessary to address cases of child sexual abuse and to protect children.

Reacting to the U.N. report in February 2014, Barbara Blaine, the president of SNAP (Survivors Network of those Abused by Priests) said it was clear that the Vatican had put the reputation of Church officials above the protection of children. "Church officials knew about it and they refused to stop it. Nothing has changed. Despite all the rhetoric from Pope Francis and Vatican officials, they refuse to take action that will make this stop," she said. The Vatican responded by saying it would examine the report - but also accused its authors of interference.

It would appear that the Catholic Church still fails to understand the depth of the spiritual damage done to the victims, families, parents and the community itself. By admitting to the gravity of spiritual harm, would in turn admit to internal failings of the faith defined institution itself. Still, the church refuses to acknowledge or understand just how profound the impact of abuse was on survivors.

Let's get back to Kelly Clark and his advocacy for ending sexual harassment and abuse. After his untimely and shocking death in 2013, the law firm he founded that enjoyed so much success in representing sex abuse victims eventually disbanded. When he died, it was as if his firm became rudderless without his steady leadership. Many of the attorneys who worked there went on to form their own practices and are involved in more sex abuse cases today ranging from churches to public schools to government institutions and individuals. Evidently, there is a lot of business to be had in the field. After all, Kelly left a well plotted road map on the subject. As I write this, I know personally of at least four law firms from the original firm involved in legal representation of this nature. They are listed at the end of this chapter.

For all his good traits, Kelly had faults and imperfections and was admittedly no saint, marrying three times. He had a colorful reputation of his own as a legislator, yet he performed important ground-breaking work in the field of sexual abuse. Later in his life, he served as an adjunct professor at George Fox University, and in 2012, received the Master's Degree in Theology from Australia's Melbourne College of Divinity. Often asked to lecture and teach effective public speaking, Kelly was frequently in demand as a speaker and writer on the topics of child abuse, law, public policy, faith, and recovery from addiction. We are all still learning from his work. I miss you, Kelly.

Below is a listing of some Oregon Law firms specializing in the field of sexual abuse, harassment and assault.

Leisel "Sam" Ruckwardt, Attorney at Law
818 SW 3rd Ave
Portland, Or 97204
sruckw@aol.com
503-274-1171 / 503-753-5575

Gilion C. Dumas
Dumas Law Group, LLC
3835 NE Hancock Street, Suite GL-B
Portland, OR 97212
www.DumasLawGroup.com
503-952-6789
Rose City Reader

Kristian Roggendorf, Esq.

5200 SW Meadows Road, Suite 150
Lake Oswego, OR 97035
Phone: 503-726-5927
Fax: 503-726-5911
Email: kr@roggendorf-law.com
Website: http://roggendorf-law.com/
Blog: http://roggendorf-law.com/category/blog/

Crew Janci, LLP, Attorneys
Peter Janci

Website: www.crewjanci.com
Phone: (888) 407-0224
Fax: (503) 467-4940
Email:info@crewjanci.com
Fremont Place II, Suite 125
1650 NW Naito Parkway
Portland, Oregon 97209-2534

The Damaging Infinite Costs of Sexual Harassment and Macy's Thanksgiving Day Parade

---

The emotional and economic costs of sexual harassment will one day be calculated in terms of actual dollars spent on payouts, workplace training programs, criminal prosecution, as well as job loss, low productivity, therapy and psychological retooling, and damaged careers for the victims. Predictably, the numbers will astound watchers as the amount could finance the upstart of many economically depressed Third World countries. Yet here in America, we continue to pay, pay, pay thinking the root cause of the problem is someone else's to handle and maybe it will just magically go away. That's the dirty underside of pay-to-play in action as society still fails its victims by ignoring the problem.

Corporate America continues to be exposed. Nike, Inc. one of America's largest makers of athletic shoes and apparel, has fired two of its top executives after reports that they contributed to a culture of inappropriate workplace conduct, including demeaning treatment of women and immigrants.

The exact reason for the expulsions was not made public for ousting of VP Jaymie Martin and brand president Trevor Edwards, who was picked as the heir apparent for CEO. This Beaverton, Oregon company is a popular employer and founded by favorite son Phil Knight, a graduate of University of Oregon, now retired. My own conversations with women who previously worked at Nike reveals that many women have quit in recent years because of their inability to rise beyond middle management positions. Maybe that wasn't the only reason for their departure. The all-male hierarchy seems to have kept women from breaking the glass ceiling at this progressive Oregon company as the power differential played hard ball once again. While many current employees at Nike strive to eliminate sexual harassment from the inside using company resources, obstacles abound. One anonymous insider stated that a quote from a top official says it all, "This company was started in a locker room and by God, it's gonna stay in a locker room" So much for trying to change behavior from the top down.

The vast dollars spent as hush money may never be revealed. But the incalculable cost to women in terms of emotional and mental wellbeing – well- that doesn't have a dollar figure attached. The lingering effects can persist for a lifetime long after the checks have been cashed, the careers restarted or slowed down and the feel-good training programs implemented by human resource agents.

A tipping point came in 2017, for whatever reason, as numerous women have accused movie producer Harvey Weinstein of rape, assault, or harassment. That action seemed to give more women courage as they tell of sexual harassment from many other high-powered men in politics, business and media. This chain reaction has set a fire that promises to burn unchecked until every single male offender in America is skewered.

Corporate America continues to be exposed. Nike, Inc. one of America's largest makers of athletic shoes and apparel, has fired two of its top executives after reports that they contributed to a culture of inappropriate workplace conduct, including demeaning treatment of women and immigrants.

The exact reason for the expulsions was not made public for ousting of VP Jaymie Martin and Brand President Trevor Edwards, who was picked as the heir-apparent for CEO. This Beaverton, Oregon company is a popular employer and founded by favorite son Phil Knight, a graduate of University of Oregon, now retired. My own conversations with women who previously worked at Nike reveals that many women have quit in recent years because of their inability to rise beyond middle management positions. Maybe that wasn't the only reason for their departure. The all-male hierarchy seems to have kept women from breaking the glass ceiling at this progressive Oregon company as the power differential played hard ball once again.

In an interview with *Variety*, actress Tara Subkoff — who made her film debut in the 1994 thriller *When the Bough Breaks*, says her professional life never fully recovered after she turned down a sexual advance from Weinstein at a premiere party around the same time.

"My reputation was ruined by false gossip, and I was called 'too difficult to work with,'" she says. "It became impossible for me to get work as an actress after this."

Actress Mira Sorvino told *The New Yorker* that an encounter with Weinstein may have blacklisted her from job opportunities. "I definitely felt iced out and that my rejection of Harvey had something to do with it," she says (businessinsider.com).

Rosanna Arquette, another actress who spoke to *The New Yorker* about alleged harassment from Weinstein, says the producer told her she was making a mistake by rejecting him. "He made things very difficult for me for years," she says.

Bill O'Reilly Fox News star made multiple sexual advances towards Juliet Huddy, a former Fox News employee, in 2011, according to a January report in the *New York Times*. When she refused, O'Reilly "began to retaliate against her both on and off air," her lawyers write in a letter to Fox News. Here's an excerpt:

Mr. O'Reilly nitpicked her work and would berate Ms. Huddy for minor mistakes, according to the letter. Mr. O'Reilly stopped preparing her for segments and would surprise her with story angles that they had not discussed. In 2013, Ms. Huddy was replaced on one segment of his show. Another segment that she was featured in, called "Mad as Hell," was canceled. She did not complain, fearing retaliation, she told current and former Fox News employees at the time.

Kellie Boyle, a former political communications consultant who says she was harassed by Roger Ailes in 1989, says the incident "soured" her dream of working in politics. Today, she runs a marketing firm with her husband. "I was really lost for a few years," Boyle tells *Fortune*. "I had my career taken away from me." Ailes denied all of the allegations against him before his death in May 2017.

Additionally, at least 60 women have accused actor Bill Cosby of rape or sexual assault, and many say the experience dealt a blow to their careers.

Andrea Constand, former director of operations of the women's basketball team at Temple University, switched to massage therapy after Cosby assaulted her in 2004, according to reports.

So, did Helen Gumpel, a former model and actress who says Cosby made sexual advances towards her during an audition for *The Cosby Show* in 1988. "I never thought of myself as a victim because I refused his advances," Gumpel said I a 2015 press conference. "But my career was a victim."

The common thread of all the previous listed testimony is evidence that harm to their careers resulted. These are famous, beautiful women who could leave other less accomplished women to think, if they can't get it to stop, then who am I to get things to change?

Some workplaces have become hostile environments shoving women out the door for greener pastures or even out of their chosen field altogether. In turn it exacts a high cost on individuals and communities, but the price is unduly shouldered by women who least can afford it. This is especially true concerning women of color and other minorities while management continues to turn a blind eye to the epidemic.

A 2008 study by the American Psychological Association found a correlation between "work withdrawal" and the aftermath of sexual harassment for black women. And in a 2016 survey of the Chicago leisure and hospitality industry, where the majority of women of color, 49 percent of housekeepers said a guest had answered the door naked or exposed themselves. The most damning result? Of those housekeepers, 56 percent said they did not feel safe returning to work after the incident (Huffingtonpost.com).

The system was failing these women. Formal report numbers were low, partly because the workers didn't believe it would make a difference to tell their stories. In fact, 43 percent of respondents said they knew someone who had reported harassment and seen nothing change.

Unfortunately, their fears are well-founded. Two-third of employees who spoke out against workplace mistreatment faced some sort of retaliation, according to a 2003 study cited by the U.S. Equal Employment Opportunity Commission. And although times are changing, they might not be changing for women in certain workplaces fast enough.

When marginalized women, particularly women of color, need solidarity, their white sisters don't often show up. My experience has shown that women usually question the woman reporting the harassment, wondering what *they* did wrong.

Fatima Goss Graves, the CEO of the National Women's Law Center, agreed, saying, "Class and race and stature play into whether someone is believed."

Ironically, the #MeToo movement was started a decade ago by black social activist Tarana Burke. However, it took Alyssa Milano, a white actress, using the hashtag for it to go viral among other white women. We've seen this before, such as in the racism of the suffragettes, FEMEN's attempts to "liberate" Muslim women despite protests, and the exclusive nature of the Women's March. When marginalized women, particularly women of color, need solidarity, their white sisters don't often show up.

Women who experience long-term sexual harassment often develop mental and emotional health issues. Failing to recognize and treat certain diseases can leave life-long effects for their futures.

Dr. Colleen Cullen, a licensed clinical psychologist at Columbia University Medical Center, notes that for victims of sexual harassment, the most common diagnoses are depression, anxiety, and even post-traumatic stress disorder (PTSD).

"An experience with sexual harassment can either trigger symptoms of depression and anxiety that are new to the person; or it can exacerbate a previous condition that may have been controlled or resolved. Patients may also see a worsening of symptoms," says Dr. Cullen. A research paper published by HHS Public Access found that sexual harassment early in one's career in particular can cause long-term depressive symptoms" (ncbi.nih.gov).

"They may feel that they did something to make this happen or egg it on in some way," says Cullen. "Embarrassment can be experienced, a fear over other people finding out. Also, particularly early in their career, a person may doubt their ability, and wonder if they weren't only hired because of their sexual value. They may question their achievements, and if they're young or new to a field, they may ask, 'Is this just what it's like in this field?' If they have nothing to compare it to, they may not have an idea of what is normal or what the appropriate recourse is." Other psychologists agree.

"Sometimes sexual harassment registers as a trauma, and it's difficult for the patient to deal with it, so what literally happens is the body starts to become overwhelmed," says Dr. Nekeshia Hammond, a licensed psychologist and the first African-American President of the Florida Psychological Association. "We call it somatizing: the mental health becomes so overwhelming one can't process it to the point of saying 'I have been traumatized' or 'I am depressed.' Essentially, it's a kind of denial that when experienced for a long state can turn into physical symptoms" (nbcnews.com).

These physical symptoms can run the gamut, manifesting as muscle aches, headaches, or even chronic physical health problems such as high blood pressure and problems with blood sugar. "In the long term, it could lead to heart issues," says Hammond.

While sexual harassment under any circumstances can wreak havoc on a victim's health, workplace harassment is a special kind of ugly. Nannina Angioni, a labor and law employment attorney who has worked on hundreds of sexual harassment cases, describes it as "slithering snake that ripples its way through a work environment causing disastrous results."

"Employees talk of having a pit in their stomach commuting to work, having anxiety, panic attacks, inexplicable fits of crying and physical manifestations of stress: hair falling out, hives, weight gain or loss, sleeplessness and lethargy," says Angioni.

Additionally, *Life Sciences Magazine* identifies six health issues that result from sexual harassment that damages women's health (livescience.com).

1. <u>Depression.</u> Many people who experience sexual harassment have feelings of self-doubt, said Amy Blackstone, a sociologist at the University of Maine. "For some people, that self-doubt turned into self-blame," she said, and victims can feel responsible for what happened. Such self-blame may have a negative effect on mental health, including promoting feelings of depression.

2. <u>Post-Traumatic Stress Disorder.</u> Many studies have found a link between experiences of sexual harassment and symptoms of post-traumatic stress disorder (PTSD), which includes re-experiencing the trauma, and avoiding people or things that may remind the victim of the harassment. In fact, women in the military who are sexually harassed are up to four times as likely to develop PTSD as women exposed to a traumatic event in combat, according to a 2015 article in the *Journal of Law and Human Behavior of the American Psychological Association.*

3. <u>Blood Pressure.</u> Researchers found a significant correlation between sexual harassment and elevated blood pressure in women. Sexual harassment may trigger the same type of physiological reactions as stress, which is thought to raise the risk of cardiovascular disease.

4. <u>Sleep Problems.</u> Sexual harassment has been linked to sleep disturbances, said Debra Borys, a psychologist with a private practice in Westwood Village, CA. This may be because the stress and anxiety of the event affects sleep

habits. For instance, victims may lie awake at night ruminating about the event, or the event may be the source of nightmares, Borys said.

5. <u>Suicide.</u> Of women who had experienced frequent, unwanted sexual touching, 15 percent said they had made suicidal attempts "often" in the past six months, compared with 2 percent of students that had not experienced sexual harassment.

6. <u>Neck Pain</u>. Sexual harassment leads to physical aches and pains, according to a Canadian study published this year that involved nearly 4,000 women. In the study, women with neck pain were 1.6 times more likely to report having experienced unwanted sexual attention.

Sexual harassment can cause emotional trauma and missed career opportunities for victims, not to mention costing them thousands in attorneys' fees and lost wages. The cost for companies is its failure to secure and keep a diversified work force as women leave as well is viewed as a loss of reputation of being a thoughtful progressive company that employees seek out. It is an affront to our American values of equality in the workplace that employers in private sector as well as governmental institutions fail to at least try to fix the problem.

The continued public sexualization of women and children is a widespread phenomenon in American culture since the arrival of the new century. It never used to be that way. My mother taught me growing up that if you appeared in your bra and panties you were half naked. Being seen half naked was not only inappropriate but akin to scandalous behavior outside your own bedroom or bathroom.

Imagine my outright disgust when I tuned on the TV to watch the Macy's 91st Annual Thanksgiving Day Parade on November 23, 2017, when shown in the background was a two-story billboard displaying two women clad only in their bras. The Victoria's Secrets billboard was strategically placed directly behind the floats with children on board and marching bands of high school students traveling down the main street in Manhattan, New York City. Billed as a family show, NBC broadcast the event that aired at 2:00 p.m. Pacific Standard Time on my local channel.

This comes at the same time when sexual assault, abuse and harassment claims by women in this country were flying off the charts. Is there any wonder why? Could it be that this singular focus was a contributing factor in accounting for the increased sexual misconduct among some men toward women? Showing women in their bras normalizes once taboo mores while at the same time encouraging male erotic fantasies of not just one female but two at the same time.

Initially, I thought it was just a mistake and that the camera angle would change once it was discovered that half-naked women were shown. Boy, was I stupid! Let me explain what I think happened, although I have not verified with NBC producers. I doubt seriously they would ever return my phone calls or emails on the subject. My objections would never register as important enough for them to consider.

In the big, rich world of TV and movies it's called *product placement*. Companies are willing to pay huge sums money to have their products displayed subtly in certain scenes in a movie or a TV show. Years ago, I learned of this and since then have been on alert for the clever subconscious messaging.

At first view I thought, "Well, isn't it lucky for Victoria's Secrets that they get that free publicity for their products." Then upon watching the entirety of the parade, no effort was ever made by the cameramen or producers to move the cameras or change the angle to hide the billboard.

NBC *Today Show* hosts Matt Lauer, Savannah Guthrie and Al Roker continued to moderate the show acting unaware the billboard even existed. Maybe the three commentators couldn't see the large-as-day, two-story billboard from their viewpoint and therefore they could have been unaware. Maybe. Or maybe one or more of them objected ahead of time but were overruled by the folks who sign their paychecks. We don't know. What I do know is NBC's *Today Show* is the wealthiest quasi-news show in America earning an estimated one-half billion dollars annually in advertising revenue, which is double that of the ABC and CBS morning shows combined.

The Victoria's Secrets larger-than-life billboard is a harsh contrast to what Americans tend to view about America's unique holiday and the image of the Thanksgiving table shown in a Norman Rockwell painting. In one of his *Four Freedoms* illustrations, Rockwell depicted a scene of a huge turkey set on a dining room table with well-behaved family members anxiously awaiting its carving. The ad slogan "we've come a long way baby" isn't what the Virginia Slims cigarette ads had in mind when targeting women to buy their products. We've come a long way, all right, since Norman Rockwell's heart-felt artistic depictions of American life.

What we learned shortly thereafter, however, was that Matt Lauer, one TV's richest celebrities was fired by executives after learning of his sexual harassment of women at NBC's *Today Show*. No wonder he didn't object to viewing women in their bras publicly – he liked it! What man doesn't? Just like the BBM's who served on the The Weinstein Company board of directors discussed earlier, the executives at NBC claimed they knew nothing of the abuse that occurred right under their noses, although many women have come forward making statements to the contrary.

I wish I had a dollar for every time I heard that said. Since these people are so rich, I have a London Bridge for sale right here on my hazelnut farm in Oregon. It's a good deal, too.

What I do know is this: corporate America and the media are complicit, guilty as hell conspirators, in the manipulation, in the promoting of sexualization of women. At the time of the initial accusations against Lauer, NBC execs claimed no knowledge of his activities despite the fact that some women previously reported them. It appears that someone is lying in order to protect who and what? Their denial raises more questions. If women are sexualized then so too are our children as they are also exposed to media culture through viewing TV, the use of the internet on cell phones and other media devices. Matt Lauer, is that what you want for your daughter? To become another TV execs' sex toy while showing your sons how to follow in your footsteps? I'm sure you would be the first to protest to the indoctrination of your own children.

When women are offered up as sexual objects, some men will view this as open season for them to fulfill their sexual fantasies and therefore act out with aggression. Hence, one of the reasons there are so many claims of sexual misconduct. Common knowledge that is backed up by research says sexualization of men and women's roles can be linked to sexual objectification.

In study after study, findings have indicated that women more often than men are portrayed in a sexual manner. According to the *American Psychological Association*, sexualization occurs when "individuals are regarded as sex objects and evaluated in terms of their physical characteristics and sexiness (e.g., dressed in revealing clothing), with bodily postures or facial expressions that imply sexual readiness." Geesh, if this is true, we women can't win for losing.

The Victoria's Secrets billboard certainly portrays women as *dressed in revealing clothing*. Furthermore, women appearing in bras is viewed a sexy, therefore sexualization exists, therefore women are objectified.

Catherine McCall, MS, LMFT, writes about the numerous studies that concluded that ample evidence exists of the sexualization of women, adolescents, and girls is evident across the media. She states in *Psychology Today*, referencing the American Psychological Association task force study in 2006: "A person is made into a thing for others' sexual use, rather than seen as a person with the capacity for independent action and decision making. Sexuality is inappropriately imposed upon a person" (psychologytoday.com).

Observing how children and adolescents have glommed onto social media through their cells phones shows us how our impressionable youth can become brainwashed despite the influence of schools, families and outside activities. In their report, the task force argues that the sexualization of young girls contributes to sexist attitudes within society and a social tolerance of sexual violence.

Tolerance of sexual violence must never, ever be accepted by any society. For far too long it appears that many women have tolerated and hidden the abuse. Not any more, as more women rise up to oppose this nastiness.

Critics may call me prudish or overly sensitive in my evaluation of the Victoria's Secrets billboard displayed on Thanksgiving Day. But I say this, there is problem in America today as evidenced by the sexual abuse of women by men. It appears that carte blanche licenses are given for advertisers to promote overt sexualization on every street corner in America where enough money is offered to buy a space from a willing seller. Yep, pay-to-play strikes again. This is a problem.

Why Now?

Women have recently realized that our rights of equality and feminism were no longer the linear ascent to heaven once promised; those aspirations have instead turned into an angry bell curve, and we're sliding down the back side.

Few issues on the planet have done more to galvanize a women's movement than the outing of the sexual mistreatment of women. What previous women's movements have failed to accomplish historically through protest, hard work, dutiful service, talent and brains -- perverted men achieved through wielding terror into vulva land. This single act has ignited women's anger into a unifying, unstoppable energy. If some degenerate men can weaponize sex, then some women in response have weaponized anger.

The 1976 phrase, "I'm mad as hell and I'm not going to take it anymore," has finally found its place in the American lexicon. To date, over 80 women have come forward with accusations against Weinstein, which in turn ignited a firestorm with initially hundreds and now thousands more women with #MeToo stories against other Hollywood elites as well as business executives and elected politicians.

It's as if God said in Her quest for justice in this post-Weinstein shakeup, "Harvey, you're gonna be My poster boy for the creation of one of the most powerful movements to grace My planet." Feminists could not have planned it any better with all their activism and messaging. Sexual misconduct, harassment and abuse has become a potent catalyst garnering America's attention, leaving other nations of the world to wonder, what the hell happened to you?

The year 2017 started with the fated optimism of the *Women's March* and ended with the heartbreak of #MeToo, which tells us something about the delicate balance if not reticence of woman's participation in her own destiny.

What's different in 2017? As observers noted -- Charlie Rose, Bill Cosby, Matt Lauer and Bill O'Reilly didn't screw with the likes of Gwyneth Paltrow, Angelina Jolie, Salma Hayek or Ashley Judd as Weinstein did. These accomplished actresses have nobly accepted their birthright as proud Gen Xer's who genetically carry a zero-tolerance attitude toward sexual harassment. True to form, these Gen Xer's independently came forward not seeking the limelight, but to confidently halt bad behavior as they saw it. But don't forget who birthed these brave women who spoke up: it was their baby boomer mothers who first screamed for gender equality in the 1970's and who through examples of their own failings infused work life values into their daughters' brains.

No worthy movement or revolution exists in a vacuum chamber as these echo boomers forge ahead to accomplish in one year what the baby boomer generation failed to accomplish in 40 years. By exposing sexual harassment, these women have also exposed the harsh reality of gender inequality in America at embarrassing levels by shaming powerful men in business and politics into actually trying to solve the problem. *Salute!*

In today's America, social power and financial power still translates into sexual power -- who has it and who doesn't. In our quest to pass progressive laws at the state and local levels that reinforce individual rights such as gay marriage, diversity inclusion, right - to-die, right-to-live, right-to-drugs (aka legalized marijuana) – citizens have demanded through the initiative vote the rights to do just about anything we want to do to ourselves or others -- still, we remain in the Dark Ages when it comes to the basic treatment of the sexes.

It's as if our laws nibbled around the edges of freedom but failed to address what really gives true freedoms we humans' desire. Women desire to be regarded as equals in the workplace because we have earned it, and we deserve it. This means equal pay for the same work, equal opportunities for promotion and equal respect regarding our unique sexuality. Keep your hands off us! We, however, live in a culture of men versus women, of rich versus poor, of us versus them, of who has the power and who doesn't in our workplace dynamic.

Why now? There are several scenarios that address why in 2017 marks the year where women have come to the harsh conclusion that gender equality is a farce. Our past is always a predictor of future events. The gauntlet has been thrown.

Marked by the election of 2016 where a woman failed to become president of the United States, where expectations ran high in America's largest population sector (women make up 54% of voting block), but blame should not be put upon Hillary Clinton for losing. Blame, if any, should be assigned as to why there were so few women candidates running for the position in the first place.

Out of a couple dozen Republicans who ran in the primary election, one woman, Carli Fiorina, was brave enough to bare her soul to the electorate. The democrat party didn't fare much better by offering up Hillary as the only viable female candidate.

With Hillary came enough baggage to sink *Titanic's* sister ship and drove enough female voters to hold their noses while they voted Republican. The puzzling election of Donald Trump to the Presidency left many women scratching their heads.

The election of Donald Trump momentarily put any hope of a revived women's movement on its heels as the double whammy of failed expectations sank further into our conflicted consciousness. So, when faced with a problem, what do women do best? We think, we plan, and we act. Barely ten weeks after the election of 2016, The Women's March on January 21, caught the attention of the world.

Gentlemen, you should not have been surprised by the Women's March, yet you were. One could say that the remarkably peaceful Women's March was an outlet for all the injustices suffered through the generations and highlighted the frustrations women felt. Although onlookers struggled to define exactly what was accomplished at the time of the March by people like myself, today I'm convinced it was an initial spark that has given a rebirth to unity among women and why now so many women have chosen to finally report sexual harassment. Women are no longer afraid because there is solidarity in numbers. We finally recognized what should have been apparent: women are a majority in America.

Things are changing. The following story hit close to home for me and my family. Patricia G. Smith is my 82-year old mother-in-law. While I have been married to her son for over 40 years, I was totally unaware of this story until she gave it to me on Christmas Eve, 2017. She wanted her story to be a part of this book. Thank you, Pat, for sharing this:

When I Was Nine Years Old

"When I was of small age, nine, my family attended a summer picnic each year. We went to a big park. Picnic was a (family) reunion. My dad's brother, George, came to it sometimes as a grown man, but he was odd and single. He was so fun to us little kids. Coming from a very large family, I really was thrilled he noticed me. One time he convinced me to go on a walk down to the creek with him.

When we got down to the creek, I realized that I hadn't told Mama where I was. So I said I had to go back to the family. George said we would soon. He just wanted a little hug and a kiss from me. I didn't want to do that so I was shy and would not and hesitated saying mama would be going home and wondered where I was. George said he would take me back soon.

After a long time it seemed to me, I gave him a quick kiss on the cheek and moved apart. I told him I had to leave. He took my hand and led to the picnic crowd. Everybody was ready to leave, and they were looking for me. I got Hell from my mom for being gone. I was so shy and embarrassed to have been bad I never told anyone about it.

Come the next year for the picnic, I was real concerned what to do. I told no one and was relieved that George wasn't there.

Another year at this same picnic, George made friends with my younger sister, Delma, not me. Then a few years after that, he made friends with another younger sister, Willa. He took Willa down to the creek. I was so afraid because uncle took her, making very friendly attempts to her. I got very afraid again so I walked carefully and eventually got mama's "ear" alone and told her to watch Willa all the time so she didn't go with uncle alone. I was okay.

Years later, Delma and I visited and I told her what George did to me. She said the same thing was done to her. Many years later Uncle

George moved to a town near ours and, married an older lady who worked in care homes.

Uncle George became a volunteer there and would put the ladies to bed, the nurse later told me. I often wondered about that.

~Pat

If the Women's March failed to galvanize a single conscious collective, the year ending #MeToo campaign captured one single behavior that broke our hearts and started a movement. The very specific act of sexual harassment would still be silent if not for the support from our sisters on all matters female which the March showed us was possible.

Even more shocking, we also were reminded that only about 22% of women hold elected positions in America, according to Center for American Women in Politics, which increased the level of frustration. The conventional wisdom told us at the time that the "women's team" lacked a strong enough bench of pinch hitters who could be regarded as Commander-in-Chief material to lead America into her rightful destiny of world influence (cawp. rutgers.edu).

Looking at the two previous mentioned glaring statistics: women make up 54% of the electorate versus 22% of women actually elected, allows us to draw a couple of alarming conclusions: 1. Women aren't running for office; and 2. Women do not vote for women -- because if we did we would hold majorities across the board in American politics today and yes, even the Presidency. Hmmmm...if it were only that simple. Gender identity politics in America doesn't work. Just ask Hillary.

Does gender identity politics work in America? Is it because that many women still remain, I'll use the word, *uncomfortable*, with seeing another woman at the lectern, sitting in the oval office, or reading the nightly news? Is this because women don't see themselves as leaders? Or is it because what's even worse is – dare I say -- women don't see other women as leaders?

As a formerly elected official at state, county and federal (nominee) level, I grappled with that very paradigm. The struggle is not with my own view of women in leadership, as much as how I have experienced women's attitudes toward other women seeking a higher position than what has historically been the norm.

In my last three campaigns for public office, roughly 93% of my political contributions came from men. There could be many reasons for this. Men own most of the businesses and earn most of the household money or men sign the checks the wives tell them to yet the official filing has a man's name attached. More likely than not I'm left to conclude that women just won't fork over the dough for another woman to win.

The Women's March through the *She Should Run* campaign has reported that more women are stepping up to run for Congressional seats citing President Donald Trump as the motivator behind the increase. The statistics are misleading, however, as the Brookings Institute concludes, 29 women Democrats targeted four Republican incumbents. (www.brookings.edu) At the most only four gains for the Democrats in Congress would be had if successful.

We need more women to run for public office. During my keynote speech at the annual 2017 Spring meeting of the Oregon Federation of Republican Women, I quoted research from CAWP, saying "women don't get elected because we don't run. We win as much as men do; the problem is we don't run." Well, ladies, times are a changing.

When voting, men will usually make up their mind quicker for their initial support of a candidate, whether it be a man or woman. Men who contribute rely on a list of explicit criteria whether it comes from their own business interests, likeable skills of the woman candidate or philosophical kinship all play a role in cracking the checkbook. Women on the other hand, and because of their very natures, take a longer amount of time to make up their minds. I believe this also correlates to the reason that women failed for so long to report their own sexual abuse. The decision to do so is wrought with too many minefields to consider along the way. A man, for instance, would not tolerate a woman groping his "junk" even one time. The power differential also comes into play.

A second harsh realization that angers women is the disparity in wages. For one deep ignorant minute did the people who set wage structure in America think that women wouldn't notice that they still are being paid at about 79 cents on the dollar of what a man makes for the same work? In my experience, it's not only the same work, but women must work harder for the same wage just to stay ahead of the double standard applied to those of us seeking a career in male-dominated fields. Arguments for less-than-premium wages are made to account for pregnancy and family care, resulting in lost time on the job and that the deeply held attitude that women somehow aren't as dedicated to their jobs because of their detached family interests. This is the time where the male boss needs to remember that he had a mother and if he's lucky, a wife. But they don't.

The argument should be the opposite! Because we have the unique anatomy that allows us to give birth, there is even more reason to elevate wages because we women are all doing this juggling act all at the same time. Admittedly, our male counterparts do not nor do they want to. Nor do I diminish the male contribution to society. I simply point out the power imbalance. Women still remain very willing to marry and have families, which gives men the same satisfaction. It's time we value women for their contribution.

Let's analyze the evolution of many of America's workplaces. They have become more than just a way to make a living and draw a paycheck. Jobs have become a haven away from home and today's workforce has demanded much more from employers aside from good pay and health benefits.

Feeling the pressure to attract and keep a skilled workforce, employers have implemented programs unheard of ten to fifteen years ago, such as flex time, telecommuting, diversity training, parental leave for men, onsite child care, employee-participated management results goal setting, gym passes, yoga classes, spruced up lunchrooms, relaxed dress codes, designer coffee and water machines -- all emulating a relaxed atmosphere to inspire and keep good employees. In essence, these overtures which now seem a necessary part of daily employment, may have inadvertently sent the wrong message of turning our workplaces into social hubs and a home away from home.

The more appeasing employers have become to their employees' needs, the more comfortable the workplaces become, the more relaxed we become as it becomes easier to cross the lines of acceptable behavior while both men and women work side by side. Boundary lines for conduct have become blurred, for both sexes. What's acceptable at, let's say the corner bar, is not acceptable at work.

Not only are women reporting sexual harassment at alarming rates, men are also admitting to it as never before.

A *New York Times/Morning Consult* poll released December 28, 2017, shows that a third of 615 men surveyed said, "they had done something at work within the past year that would qualify as objectionable behavior or sexual harassment." The survey also concluded that many of the men lied when failing to admit if they engaged in such activities.

This first-of-its-kind survey reveals never-before-admitted information from men, about men and their workplace activities. The fact that it was even conducted tells us something is amiss regarding the treatment of women at work. It's interesting to wonder if the same survey was performed on a yearly basis what the results would yield, say, ten years from now.

How we move forward to solve sexual harassment and assault in our workplace is a problem that can be remedied if we all contribute. It deserves more than just a cursory look. Women have led on this issue by exposing it; let's implore men to walk by our sides and become our helpmates to further solve it.

Workplace sexual harassment has taken root in American society, poisoning employment cultures in every single sector. Left unchanged, the repercussions will leave lasting scars that hurt not only our souls but the bottom line as well. Like an infection untreated medically, let's not allow sexual harassment to fester; let's treat it and eradicate it.

So, getting back to the original question, Why Now? At the time of the publication of this book, not all the answers we seek will be disclosed. It has not yet been "decided" if the sexual harassment reveal is only a temporary movement or if it is indeed the vehicle to spur a revolution toward true gender equality. In the end, it remains the responsibility of the participants -— women -- to show leadership.

Experts who have written about this occurrence also question its effigy. "I can't explain how these things get started," says Brian Balogh, a historian at the University of Virginia's Miller Center on Public Affairs. "But this is a real moment." (USAToday.com)

Balogh also observes that some fear has eased as women have become braver.

Small changes can make a big difference, said Catharine A. MacKinnon in her book entitled Butterfly Politics, published by Harvard University Press (hup.harvard.edu). MacKinnon explains the minuscule motion of a butterfly's wings can trigger a tornado half a world away, according to chaos theory. Under the right conditions, small simple actions can produce large complex impacts.

The *butterfly effect* can animate political activism and advance equality socially and legally, she contends. Seemingly insignificant actions, through collective recursion, can intervene in unstable systems to produce systemic change, according to her website. Thinking of it as a *butterfly moment* gives credence to the theory that small incremental happenings together can contribute to big ones. MacKinnon has had a long career as a pioneer of legal theory and practice and is an activist for women's rights.

In all fairness to the previous generations of women who endured sexual abuse, harassment and rape and who chose to remain silent, they should not be criticized. The 1970's or '80's, for instance, did not employ the social megaphone of Facebook, Twitter, Pinterest, LinkedIn, Instagram or any other social media platform. This source of instant communication, until recently, was lacking as a tool to shine a light on the behavior. This immediate media structure in place today gives courage for women to rebel in numbers and likewise be affirmed in numbers. By nature, women like to talk and share. Unlike men who tend not to discuss their emotions openly with their tribe, women see the exchange as healing. Previously, when women talked about workplace sexual harassment, it was done so privately, among themselves.

This newer means of communication is a pathway to talk to each other *en masse*. Talking about it, validates it for women. Social media can never be responsible for the birth of a revolution any more than Paul Revere's trusty steed can be as he dashed through the night shouting, "The British are coming," but just as effective, it can help spread the message.

Another breakthrough 2017 study comes from George-town University Institute for Women, Peace and Security in a first-of-its-kind measure of women's wellbeing worldwide. The WPS Index offers a comprehensive measure of women's welfare by capturing both peace and security—and women's inclusion and justice. Shockingly, the United States ranks 22 out of 153 countries in this comprehensive evaluation (giwps.gerogetown. edu). Not surprisingly, countries like Germany, Norway, Finland, and Iceland far outrank American women in employment, discrimination, and elective positions. The U.S finds itself on par with Croatia with less than one in five women to elected positions. "While countries in much of the world have boosted women's representation, (in elected positions) through some type of quota, the United States has not. At current rates of progress, according to the Center for American Women in Politics, it will take more than a century to reach gender parity." What this says about elect-ing a woman president is unclear and open for debate. One can only speculate that America is further away from electing a female Commander-in-Chief than many of us, including me, had hoped.

On the violence front, the United States ranks 66th on the WPS Index security dimension due to rates of intimate partner violence that are more than 10 percentage points above the mean for developed countries. U.S. society faces a unique crisis of lethal violence against women, given the intersections between domestic abuse and the wide-spread availability of firearms. The next logical

question to ask is this: does an attitude of inflicting domestic violence in the home then naturally follow its way into the workplace
and manifest itself in the form of sexual harassment and abuse?

While the United State ranks high in the areas of cell phone
use, education and financial inclusion, it has work to be done in
other areas. For instance, the United States has not passed a con-
stitutional amendment barring discrimination against women
nor is it a signatory to the United Nations Convention on the
Elimination of All Forms of Discrimination against Women. It
is also notable that the United States has no legal mandate for
equal pay. The gender wage gap in full-time employment averages
20 cents on the dollar and is much wider for non-white women.
The United States and Papua New Guinea are the only countries
without legally guaranteed paid maternity leave. Moreover, the
lack of childcare and paid maternity leave make the United States
an outlier among rich countries.

The study uses four dimensions with eleven criteria for its
measurements. This fascinating study can be found at https://
giwps.georgetown.edu/the-index/ and is worth the read.

Accounting for what we just learned about women's ranking
worldwide, change doesn't come from being satisfied with the status quo – real change, revolutionary change – doesn't come from
being happy but comes from being miserable. Being subject to
sexual harassment, abuse and even rape is a continual devaluing
of people's beliefs, principles and affirmations. The current status
in America's workforce of discounting even the slightest of sexual
mistreatment claims, is a warning shot across the bow to the powerful captains of industry and politics to do something. The continued failure to listen and act could result in an American version
of a figurative storming of a French Bastille prison for not doing
the right thing. You have been warned. Payoffs for pay-to-play

will hopefully reveal the participants, exposing the ugliness even further.

Unfortunately, the mere accusation of sexual misconduct has left many men wondering in their workplaces if they will be next, even they have no reason to be concerned. The mere allegation, whether true or false, can harm a good man's reputation, leave him unemployed and potentially ruin his family life. The defense of sexual harassment is to deny it happened which in essence calls the accuser a liar. Oftentimes, proof is hard to find. It is even harder to deny.

2018 will undoubtedly see the beginning of a confusing shift in workplace relationships between men and women. This is happening while at the same time we so desperately desire the fond connections between the sexes that enables a working team to prosper. Ignoring sexual harassment will serve to further divide us. Establishing workplace rules and codes of behaviors will go a long way to build trust and success.

Real-life scenarios have been played out publicly in Roy Moore's failed run for the U.S. Senate in Alabama, President Trump's presidency and even the resignation of Senator Al Franken, who said he doesn't remember the abuse happening or he remembers it differently. Innocent men could become unwilling casualties. Efforts to clean up some work places in America's corporations, industries and government institutions must happen without delay. So how do we protect the innocent while at the same time cleaning up the mess?

That is the question human resource managers and business leaders should be asking. The time has passed where reasonable people ignore the potential for abuse right under their noses.

EEOC says half of women are harassed at work, based on reports. Many women don't report harassment so the actual number is anybody's guess. But know this, women are so done. Sexual harassment of women has always existed. What's different now is that we are exposing it through the incredible leadership voluntarily presented by women. Where we go from here is anybody's guess in trying to end sexual harassment, abuse and mistreatment of people on our job sites. It's a painful process, like peeling off a scab that reveals more bleeding, but we will eventually heal. Sexual harassment should be regarded as the last bastion of slavery in America. We need all hands-on deck to eradicate it.

CONCLUSION:

Where Do We Go from Here? Helpful Resources People Can Use

—•◦•—

The aftermath of historic numbers of sexual harassment accusations have left many wondering what's next. The process has started. Now, we all must follow through to ensure the demise of sexual harassment. We must stay committed to helping every single person who has suffered abuse. We will develop a road map for success that must be followed even on days when we are too tired or exhausted to care anymore.

Fury and anger are no longer a cause for shame as it was for the actresses who first came forward to initially expose this nasty beast, aka Harvey Weinstein. Some of these same actresses - a group of women who have a loud bully pulpit by virtue of their fame and profession - protested at the January 2018 Golden Globe Awards show with actions of solidarity - by dressing in black; words of condemnation -- emphasizing the fact that *only* men were nominated for Best Director category; and examples of leadership - introducing #MeToo founder Tarana Burke to the world to stop the scourge. They must continue in these efforts to ensure real change not just for them but for all the women who don't have a voice and remain invisible.

Oprah Winfrey amplified the movement's success with her inspiring speech that captivated the nation at that iconic awards show when she accepted the Cecil B. DeMille's Lifetime Achievement Award, the first black woman ever to receive it. There comes a time in history when words should be remembered if not immortalized. In part, she said,

"...it's not just a story affecting the entertainment industry. It's one that transcends any culture, geography, race, religion, politics, or workplace. So I want tonight to express gratitude to all the women who have endured years of abuse and assault because they, like my mother, had children to feed and bills to pay and dreams to pursue. They're the women whose names we'll never know. They are domestic workers and farm workers. They are working in factories and they work in restaurants and they're in academia, engineering, medicine, and science. They're part of the world of tech and politics and business. They're our athletes in the Olympics and they're our soldiers in the military.

For too long, women have not been heard or believed if they dare speak the truth to the power of those men. But their time is up. Their time is up.

...so I want all the girls watching here, now, to know that a new day is on the horizon! And when that new day finally dawns, it will be because of a lot of magnificent women, many of whom are right here in this room tonight, and some pretty phenomenal men, fighting hard to make sure that they become the leaders who take us to the time when nobody ever has to say - "Me Too"- again."

Many of us assume that just because sexual harassment has been: 1. exposed publicly, and 2. lawsuits filed and settled, that equates to a change of behavior toward sexual abuse or harassment at institutions or workplaces. Concluding those two actions will solve the problem can lull a once-alert public into complacency. This thinking assumes that other abusers who haven't been "caught" have altered their behavior to coincide with societal outrage. Nothing is further from the truth. If that were so, the Catholic Church would be lawsuit free and we know that is not the case as depicted in the chapter on the Catholic Priest Sex Scandal where in 2017, the Australian Royal Commission identified over 4,400 current abusive priests. Presently, there are at least three lawsuits against the Portland Archdiocese. Let us be ever vigilant in watching over and protecting women and children and those in powerless positions. We must continue to identify, support and encourage victims to come forward and perpetrators to change behavior or suffer criminal circumstances.

My concluding thought is made by a poet and philosopher, "The world is dying, and we need a major *revolution of the heart* to empower everyone to step forward and start doing the work of reconstruction and re-creation that is now desperately needed," wrote Andrew Harvey in his book, entitled *Evolutionary Relationships: The Seven Requirements of Love*.

The first and most important need for people subjected to harassment or assault is having an immediate place to turn. This is a short list and certainly is not a complete list, but there are resources you can turn to.

BetterBrave

BetterBrave provides a thorough guide to identifying and dealing with sexual harassment, including information on reporting it to HR and seeking legal counsel. www.betterbrave.com.

Equal Employment Opportunity Commission (EEOC)

The U.S. Equal Employment Opportunity Commission (EEOC) is the government agency responsible for enforcing federal laws that make it illegal to sexually harass anyone in the workplace. 1-800-669-4000. www.eeoc.gov/index.cfm. https://www.eeoc.gov/laws/types/sexual_harassment.cfm

Equal Rights Advocates

Equal Rights Advocates is a nonprofit legal organization dedicated to protecting and expanding economic and educational access and opportunities for women. They provide a toll-free multi-lingual advice and counseling line where you can receive advice and information on your legal rights. All calls are confidential. 1-800-839-4372, www.equalrights.org. https://www.equalrights.org/wp-content/uploads/2013/11/KYR_SexHarassWk-v3.pdf

Lean In

Women in over 150 countries have joined the Lean In community. Read their newly created advice, information and support for harassment survivors and for anyone who wants to help. www.leanin.org/sexual-harassment/

National Domestic Violence Hotline

The National Domestic Violence Hotline provides lifesaving tools and immediate support to enable victims to find safety and live lives free of abuse. www.thehotline.org.

RAINN, Rape, Abuse & Incest National Network

RAINN provides information and a 24/7 confidential hotline, staffed by people who are trained to help in matters of sexual harassment or assault. 1-800-656.HOPE (4673) http://online.rainn.org/

Women in Film Helpline

Women in Film has launched a Sexual Harassment Help Line, an integrated program to refer victims of harassment to designated mental health counselors, law enforcement professionals, and civil and criminal lawyers and litigators. 1-323-545-0333, www. womeninfilm.org.

50/50 By 2020

50/50 by 2020 is a movement of women, people of color and LGBTQ members of the entertainment industry, advocating for leadership and hiring practices that reflect the reality of our audiences to inspire authentic content creation and safer workplaces by the end of this decade. https://5050by2020.com/

Oregon Abuse Advocates & Survivors in Service, OASSIS

OASSIS is building a movement that empowers communities to prevent child sexual abuse and help survivors live full, healthy and joyful lives. http://oaasisoregon.org/.

Survivors Network of those Abused by Priests, SNAP.

SNAP started as a support network for survivors of priest abuse but now includes survivors of abuse within any trusted institution. http://www.snapnetwork.org/.

Male Survivor

Male survivor helps men who've been sexually abused, assaulted, or raped, 24/7/365. http://www.malesurvivor.org/index.php.

It's On Us

If you've experienced sexual assault on college campuses and need crisis support, please call National Sexual Assault Hotline at 1-800-656-HOPE (4673) or visit their website 24/7. <u>www. it'sonus.org</u>.

Afterword

This book came into being because of my undying devotion for justice in the treatment of women in American society. My dual careers in the political and business worlds with good men at my side has given me the desire to elevate women into positions of equality. I know it's possible. By exposing sexual harassment and abuse against all disempowered people will serve for the betterment of our culture as we move forward to a higher spiritual plane. By exposing the how, what and why of sex crimes will hopefully move our society toward living fully and completely without fear.

The personal stories sprinkled throughout this book were contributions made by women who wish to remain anonymous for fear of reprisal, yet wanted to contribute to this body of work. Their names and identities are kept by me for safekeeping. They will forever live in my heart.

My gratitude as well as admiration go to you all for your courage to retell and relive the horrors inflicted upon you by abusers. Your words will live long so other women will learn from your experiences as we all create a safer society where women can truly become equals. Thank you.

Tootie Smith

About the Author

Tootie Smith is a speaker, an author and the president of two corporations. As a self-described life-long recovering political addict, she has been an observer, writer and star player during America's most tempestuous social times. As such, she has been an outspoken voice for the underdog. In her book, *"Pay-to-Play: Sexual Harassment American Style,"* she presents a logical yet passionate approach to these issues plaguing the U.S. Tootie identifies the reasons why harassment issues are now so prominent with alarming historical details, institutional how-to's to fix the problem and personal stories never before heard. As an underdog in a political system rife with corruption, she's become an advocate in order to advance women into positions of strength in their workplaces.

Tootie's political and business careers are speckled with triumphs as well as defeats earning her respect from both sides of the political aisle. "Politics is business and business is politics," is her mantra as her speeches entertains and educates with practical advice.

As a self-proclaimed political junkie, meriting decades of public service, she served as an elected official, lobbyist and volunteer.

Her writing career started in junior high school writing for the school paper. She was editor of her high school newspaper and year book while simultaneously employed as a sports correspondent for the city weekly newspaper. Through the decades, she penned newsletters, magazine articles, messaging for business and political campaigns, was a newspaper editor and an author of fiction books.

She went on to become one of the most successfully elected Republican women in Oregon, a state dominated by democrats. Whether it's negotiating ownership with the US Army Corps of Engineers in Washington, D.C., or ensuring the dog shelter is fiscally sound in her local county, Tootie has earned a reputation as a go-getter and tireless advocate for causes she pursues.

During her service as a state legislator, her colleagues dubbed her "spark plug" because of her ability to take on the media during press conferences. Tootie has been bestowed dozens of distinguished service awards in the fields where she was elected and most recently Mt. Hood Community College's "50 Most Notable Graduates in the last 50 years," maintains an active toolbox of how-to's and is never at a loss to share a quip that is sure to even the playing field for even the most novice wanna-be. Her approach is refreshingly nonpartisan and honest, prompting her colleagues to refer to her as "straight shooter."

Her dual track of political and business careers started in 1988 and culminated into many "firsts." She was the first women elected, ever and since, to House District 18 in Oregon State Legislature; first Republican woman ever elected to Clackamas

County Board of Commissioners; and only the second Republican women to win the primary for Congress in Congressional District 5. Tootie is a graduate from Concordia University, Portland, Oregon, in Management and Business Communication, cum laude, journalism minor.

She is a past business owner of a bed and breakfast inn for 14 years in small town Oregon, a beekeeper, living on the hazelnut farm that her parents purchased as a strawberry farm in 1959 where she and her siblings grew into adults learning a strong work ethic. As a daughter, wife, mother, aunt and friend, she is grateful for the extended family and the love it provides.

Her presentations bleed with humor, practical advice and, yes, tell the real reason why women should run for political office. Learn from Tootie why women are poised to handle the new leadership universe. Learn how to keep from sliding down the corporate glass cliff to popping the lid off the glass ceiling; from winning State House to winning the White House.

To learn more about Tootie, visit tootiesmith.com

References

Sexual Harassment Defined

1. Rowe, Mary. Saturn's Rings (1975)
2. Brownmiller, Susan. In Our Time: Memoir of a Revolution. 2000
3. Bowers, Toni; Hook, Brian. "Hostile work environment: A manager's legal liability," Tech Republic. October 22, 2002. Retrieved on March 3, 2012.
4. https://www.eeoc.gov/laws/types/sexual_harassment.cfm
5. http://www.stopvaw.org/quid_pro_quo_sexual_harassment
6. Paludi, Michele Antoinette; Barickman (1991). Academic and Workplace Sexual Harassment. SUNY Press. pp. 2–5. ISBN 0-7914-0829-9.
7. *The Economic and Career Effects of Sexual Harassment on Working Women*, Heather McLaughlin, Christopher Uggen, Amy Blackstone, First Published May 10, 2017 Research Article.
8. Larsen, S.E. and Fitzgerald, L.F. 2010. "PTSD symptoms and sexual harassment: The role of attributions and perceived control." *Journal of Interpersonal Violence*, 26, 2255-2567.

9. https://www.psychologytoday.com/blog/presence-mind/201704/what-do-psychologists-say-about-sexual-harassment.

10. Paludi, Michele Antoinette; Barickman (1991). Academic and Workplace Sexual Harassment. SUNY Press. pp. 2–5. ISBN 0-7914-0829-9.

11. https://www.avclub.com/patrick-stewart-calls-on-men-to-take-responsibility-for-1820544494

From Hollywood to Congress: Then and Now

1. https://www.axios.com/harvey-weinstein-accused-rape-harassment-2495224169.html

2. https://www.nytimes.com/2017/10/05/us/harvey-weinstein-harassment-allegations.html

3. https://www.newyorker.com/news/news-desk/why-didnt-manhattan-da-cyrus-vance-prosecute-the-trumps-or-harvey-weinstein

4. Hirsch, Foster, *The Boys From Syracuse: The Shuberts' Theatrical Empire* New York, Cooper Square Press, 2000

5. http://variety.com/2017/film/features/casting-couch-hollywood-sexual-harassment-harvey-weinstein-1202589895/

6. *Get Happy: The Life of Judy Garland*, by Gerald Clark.

7. http://www.dailymail.co.uk/news/article-3882442/How-obsessed-Alfred-Hitchcock-tried-ruin-Tippi-Hedren-s-career-refused-succumb-sexual-demands.html

8. Hedren, Tippi, *Tippi, A Memoir*, New York, Harper Collins Publishers, 2016

9. http://www.dailymail.co.uk/tvshowbiz/article-2251425/
    Tippi-Hedren-tells-Alfred-Hitchcock-turned-sexual-pred-
    ator-tried-destroy-her.html Hedren, Tippi, *Tippi, A Mem-
    oir*, New York, Harper Collins Publishers, 2016

10. https://www.washingtonpost.com/investigations/eight-
    women-say-charlie-rose-sexually-harassed-them--with-
    nudity-groping-and-lewd-calls/2017/11/20/9b168de8-
    caec-11e7-8321-481fd63f174d story.
    html?utm_term=.0c454b277cff

11. ABC affiliate, KATU 2, *News This Morning*, Nov 6, 2017

12. https://www.theatlantic.com/entertainment/
    archive/2017/11/all-the-angry-ladies/545042/

The Power Behind Weaponized Sex: Why Do Men Rape?

1. *Psychology Today*, Thomas J Leeper, Ph.D. "Means, Motive,
    and Opportunity: Addressing violence…" Dec 15, 2012
    Internet.

2. https://www.psychologytoday.com/
    blog/the-social-thinker/201711/
    are-men-socialized-prey-women

3. https://www.psychologytoday.com/blog/cutting-edge-
    leadership/201711/the-minds-powerful-sexual-preda-
    tors-how-power-corrupts

4. Bendahan, S., Zehnder, C., Pralong, F.P., & Antonakis,
    J. (in press). Leader corruption depends on power and
    testosterone. The Leadership Quarterly.

5. https://www.psychologytoday.
    com/blog/presence-mind/201704/
    what-do-psychologists-say-about-sexual-harassment

Legislating Morality

1. https://www.cga.ct.gov/2003/olrdata/jud/rpt/2003-R-0376.htm
2. http://apps.rainn.org/policy/compare/crimes.cfm
3. Michelle J. Anderson, *"Marital Immunity, Intimate Relationships, and Improper Inferences: A New Law on Sexual Offenses by Intimates,"* 54 HASTINGS L.J. 1465, 1478 (2003)
4. http://www.womenslawproject.org/wp-content/uploads/2016/04/Rape-and-Sexual-Assault-in-the-Legal-System-FINAL.pdf
5. Gabriel, Trip (29 August 1993). *"The Trials of Bob Packwood."* The New York Times Retrieved 7 October 2014.
6. *Seelye, Katharine Q. (September 8, 1995). "The Packwood Case: The Overview; Packwood Says he is Quitting as Ethics Panel Gives Evidence." The New York Times.* Retrieved October 11, 2017.
7. http://thehill.com/blogs/floor-action/house/362036-women-democrats-leading-sexual-harassment-discussion-in-congress
8. http://www.heritage.org/constitution/#!/articles/1/essays/67/appropriations-clause

The Folly of Sexual Harassment Training

1. https://www.elitedaily.com/p/sexual-harassment-in-politics-is-a-problem-these-politicians-are-taking-a-stand-against-it-3073691
2. https://www.elitedaily.com/p/sexual-harassment-in-politics-is-a-problem-these-politicians-are-taking-a-stand-against-it-3073691

3. https://www.vox.com/policy-and-politics/2017/11/2/16597574/sexual-harassment-training-senate

4. https://www.eeoc.gov/eeoc/task_force/harassment/upload/report.pdf

5. https://www.vox.com/science-and-health/2017/10/24/16498674/corporate-harassment-trainings-dont-work

6. *"Harassment Trainings: A Content Analysis,"* Elizabeth Tippet, Berkley Journal of Employment & Labor Law (Forthcoming 2018)

7. https://www.eeoc.gov/eeoc/task_force/harassment/upload/report.pdf

8. https://doi.org/10.1177/0891243217704631

9. https://www.vox.com/science-and-health/2017/10/24/16498674/corporate-harassment-trainings-dont-work

10. http://digitalcommons.law.yale.edu/cgi/viewcontent.cgi?article=5773&context=fss_papers

11. https://www.npr.org/2017/12/01/567012522/transcript-paul-ryans-full-interview-with-nprs-steve-inskeep

12. https://www.care.org/newsroom/press/press-releases/new-global-poll-significant-share-men-believe-expecting-intimate

The Language We Use Equals the Deeds We Do

1. "The Economic and Career Effects of Sexual Harassment on Working Women," Heather McLaughlin, Christopher Uggen, Amy Blackstone, First Published May 10, 2017 Research Article.

2. https://www.washingtonpost.com/posteverything/wp/2016/10/08/many-men-talk-like-donald-trump-in-private-and-only-other-men-can-stop-them/?utm_term=.306e64b365cd

3. Megyn Kelly: "Now We Need Men as Our Allies," online, Oct 19, 2017.

4. https://www.psychologytoday.com/blog/happiness-and-the-pursuit-leadership/201610/whats-wrong-locker-room-talk.

5. Baumeister R. F., & Leary M. R. (1995). "*The need to belong: Desire for interpersonal attachments as a fundamental human motivation*." Psychological Bulletin, 117, 497-529.

6. https://www.psychologytoday.com/blog/happiness-and-the-pursuit-leadership/201610/whats-wrong-locker-room-talk

7. https://www.nytimes.com/interactive/2017/12/28/upshot/sexual-harassment-survey-600-men.html?emc=edit_nn_20171228&nl=morning-briefing&nlid=83903906&te=1

8. Jackson Katz filmmaker activist and educator Fortune online Valentina Oct 18, 2017, talk at MVP Mentors in Violence Prevention.

Catholic Priest Sex Scandal

1. http://crewjanci.com/our-approach-your-healing-is-our-main-concern/tribute-to-attorney-kelly-clark/   https://www.bostonglobe.com/metro/obituaries/2017/12/19/lawbernard/PBOOOaMLW783ylMI1L6pzO/story.html

2. https://www.alternet.org/story/146920/what's_really_behind_the_catholic_church's_sexual_abuse_problem

3. https://www.theguardian.com/australia-news/2017/feb/07/catholic-church-doesnt-understand-toll-of-child-sexual-abuse-says-us-priest

4. http://www.snapnetwork.org/australia_royal_commission_recommends_sweeping_child_safety_changes_in_catholic_church_victims_respond

5. http://www.cnn.com/2017/12/14/asia/australia-child-abuse-commission-recommendations/index.html

6. https://www.alternet.org/story/146920/what's_really_behind_the_catholic_church's_sexual_abuse_problem

7. http://www.iupui.edu/~womrel/REL301%20Women/womens%20ordination%20movement_Catholic%20church.pdf

8. http://www.bbc.com/news/world-europe-26044852

9. http://www.worldreligionnews.com/issues/is-the-catholic-church-experiencing-exponential-growth-or-declining

The Damaging Infinite Costs of Sexual Harassment and Macy's Thanksgiving Day Parade

1. http://www.businessinsider.com/12-women-who-say-sexual-harassment-cost-them-their-careers-2017-11

2. https://www.huffingtonpost.com/entry/workplace-sexual-harassment_us_5a26ca50e4b0f104475e23cf

3. https://www.ncbi.nlm.nih.gov/pmc/articles/PMC3227029/

4. https://www.nbcnews.com/better/health/hidden-health-effects-sexual-harassment-ncna810416

5. https://www.livescience.com/16949-sexual-harassment-health-effects.html.

6. https://www.psychologytoday.com/blog/overcoming-child-abuse/201203/the-sexualization-women-and-girls

Why Now?

1. http://www.cawp.rutgers.edu/women-elective-office-2017

2. https://www.brookings.edu/blog/fixgov/2017/10/25/inning-two-will-2018-be-a-wave-election/

3. https://www.usatoday.com/story/news/2017/11/21/weinstein-case-fallout-why-now-why-never-before-rose-spacey-cosby-trump/884385001/

4. http://www.hup.harvard.edu/catalog.php?isbn=9780674416604

5. https://giwps.georgetown.edu/the-index/

www.ingramcontent.com/pod-product-compliance
Lightning Source LLC
Chambersburg PA
CBHW020245290326
41930CB00038B/390